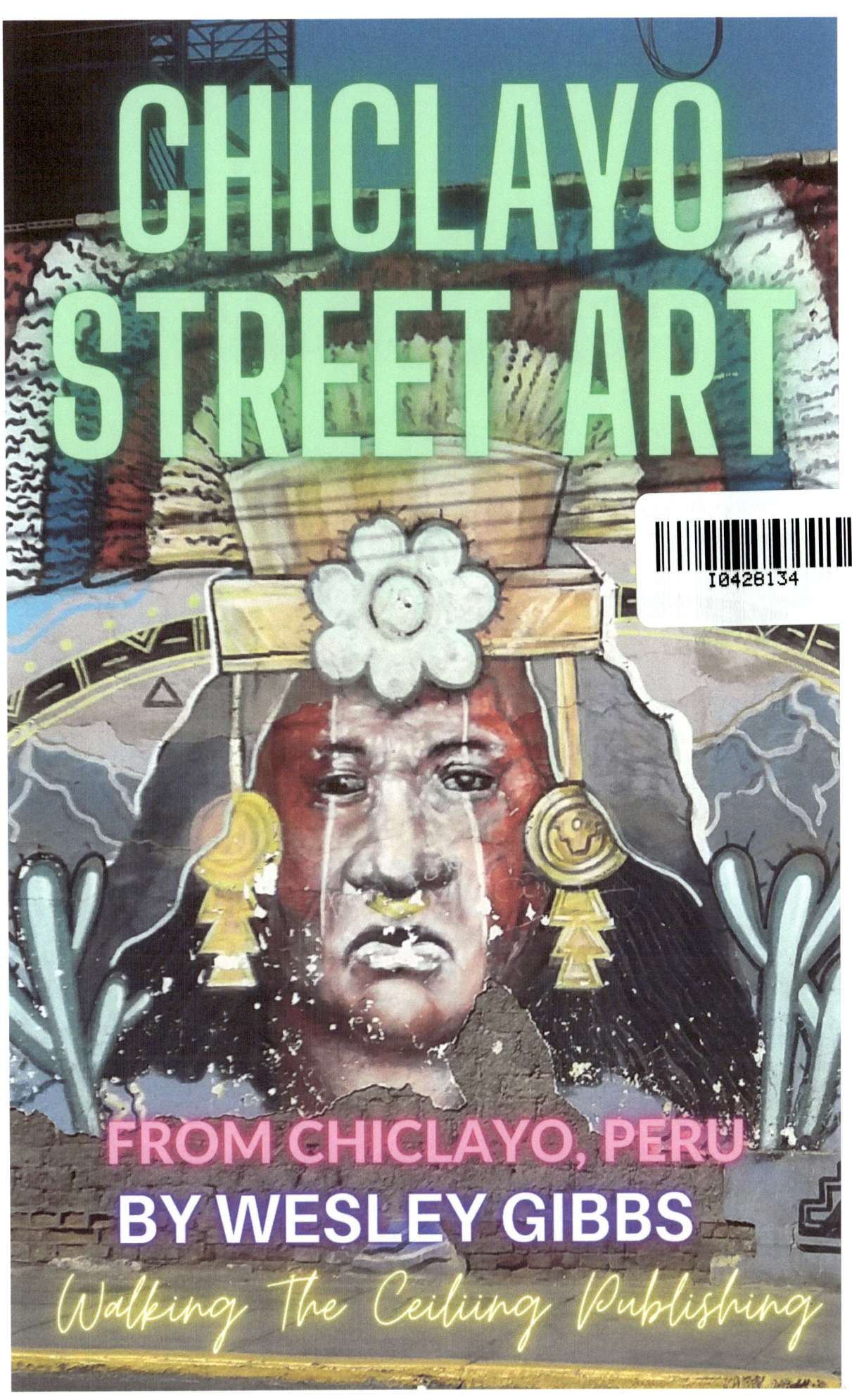

CHICLAYO STREET ART

FROM CHICLAYO, PERU
BY WESLEY GIBBS
Walking The Ceiling Publishing

Chiclayo Street Art

Photos From Chiclayo, Peru

By Wesley Gibbs

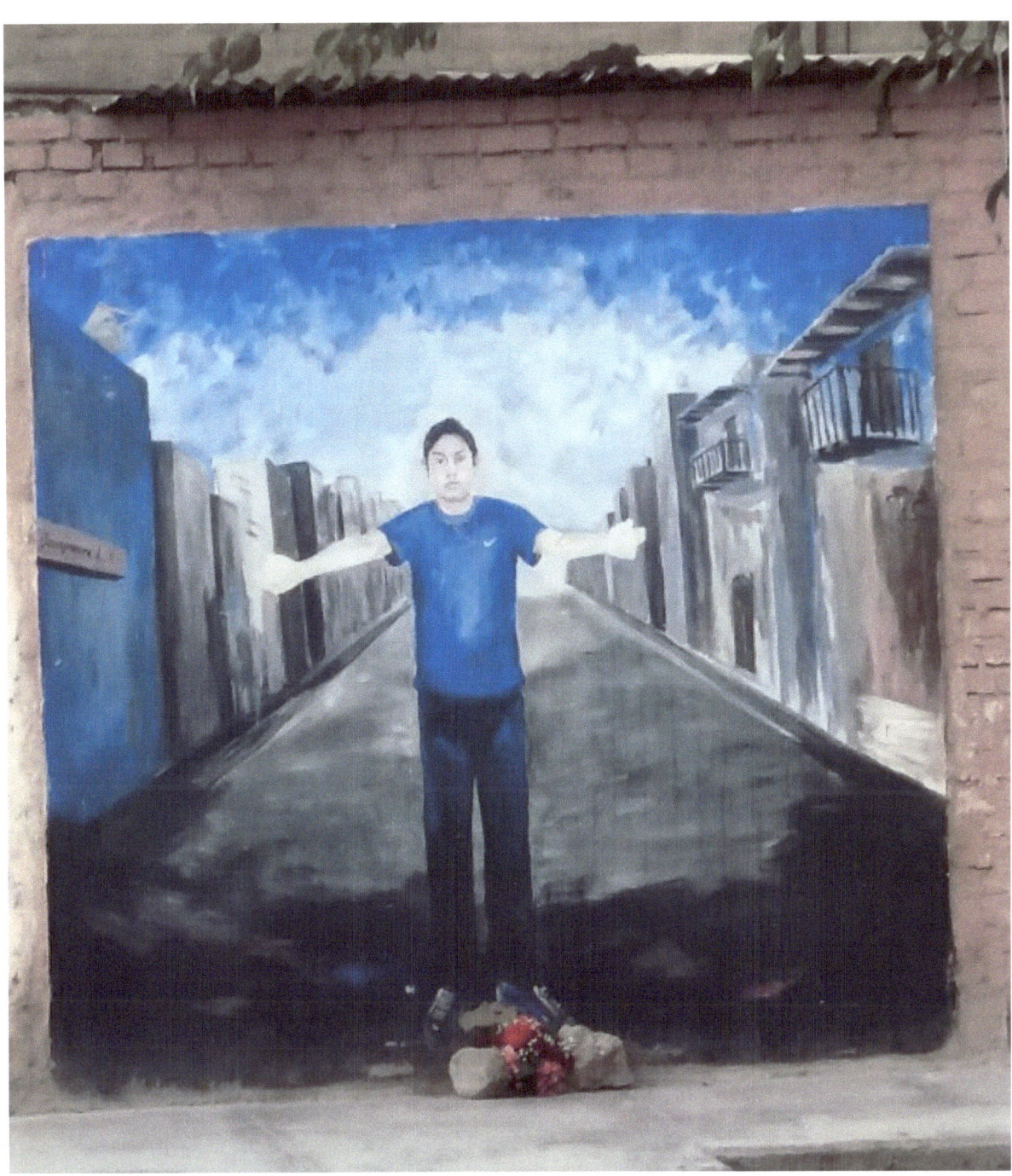

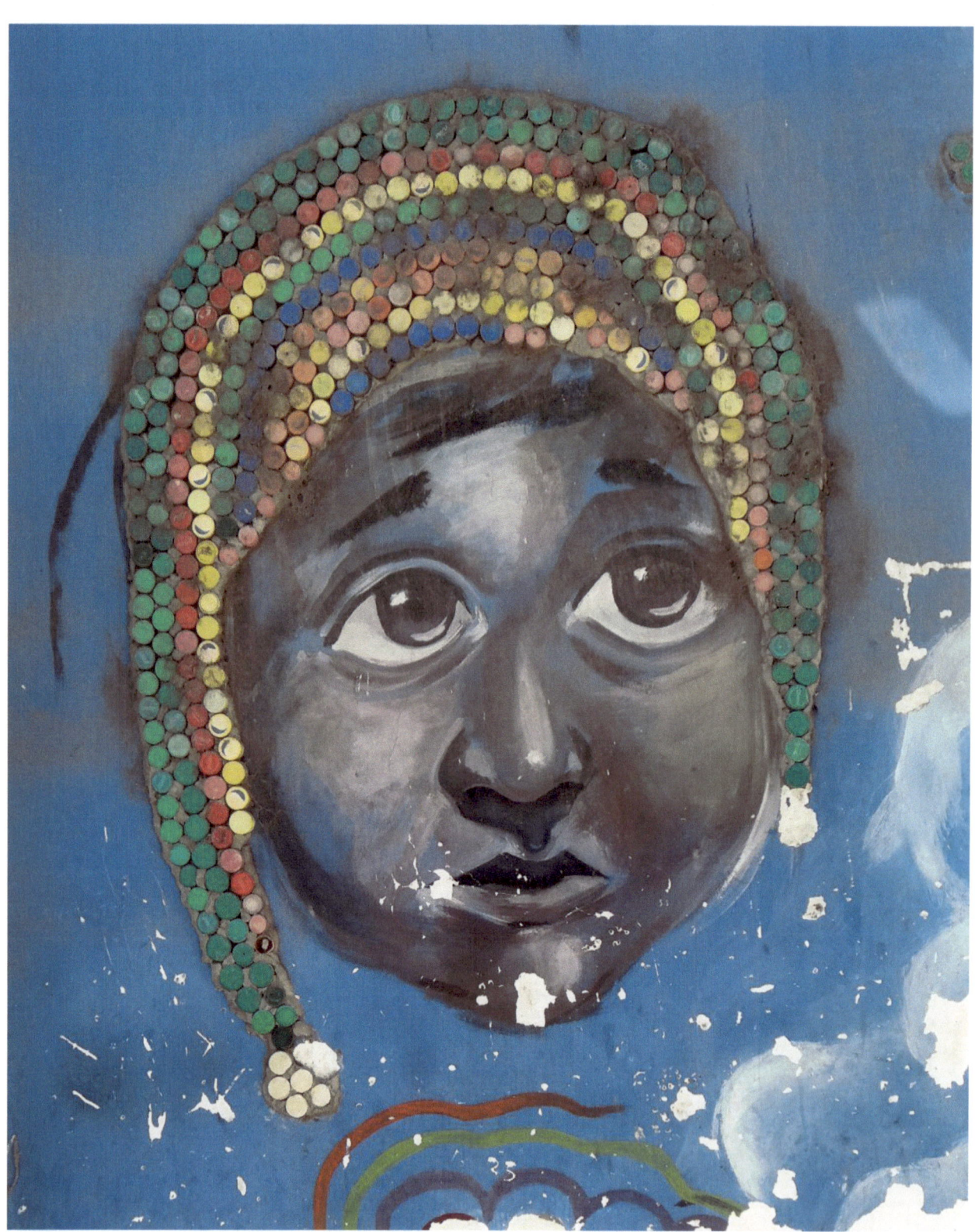

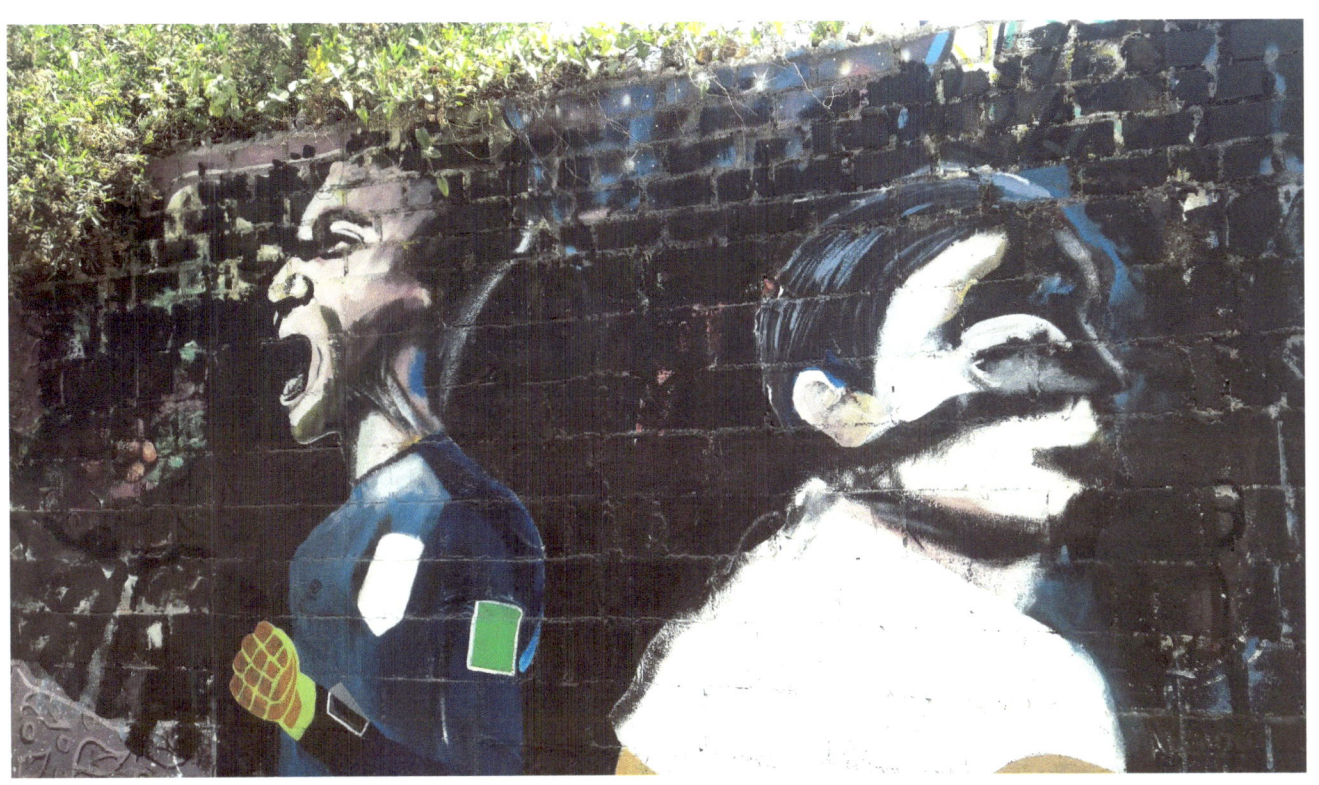
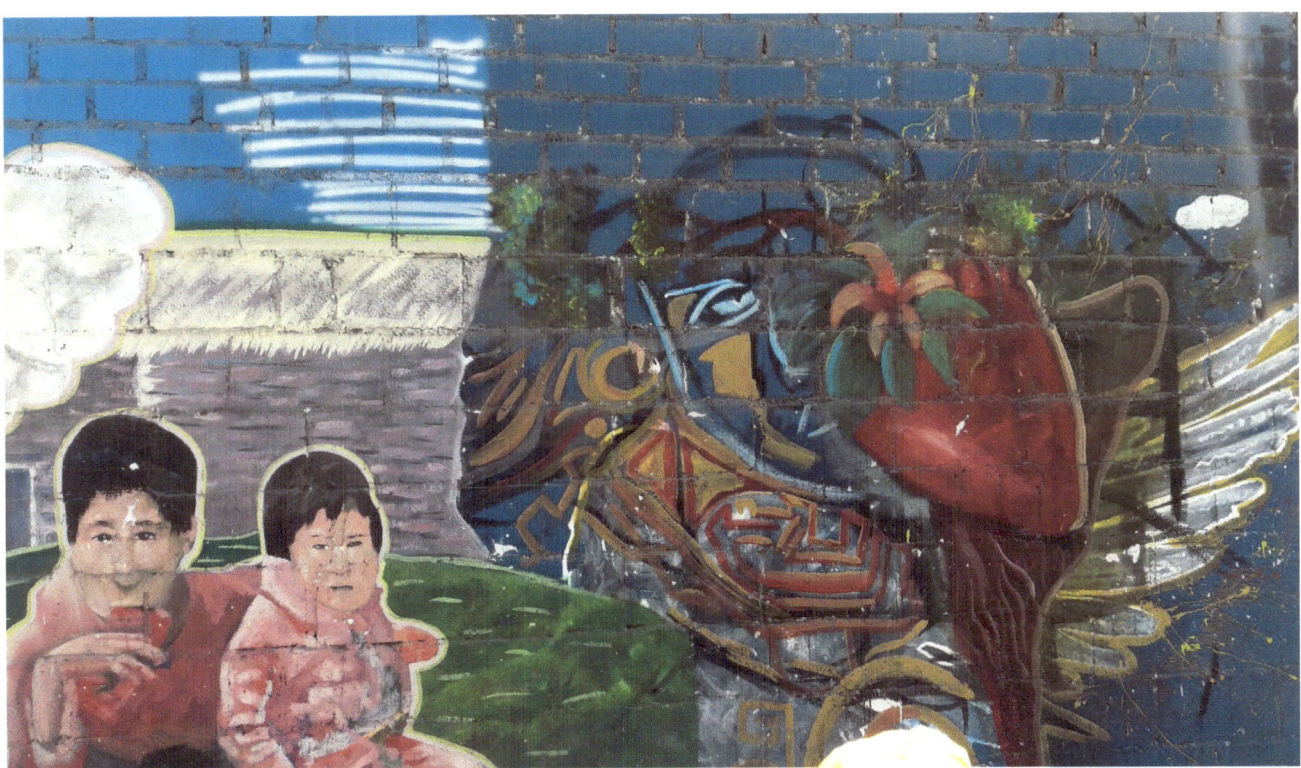

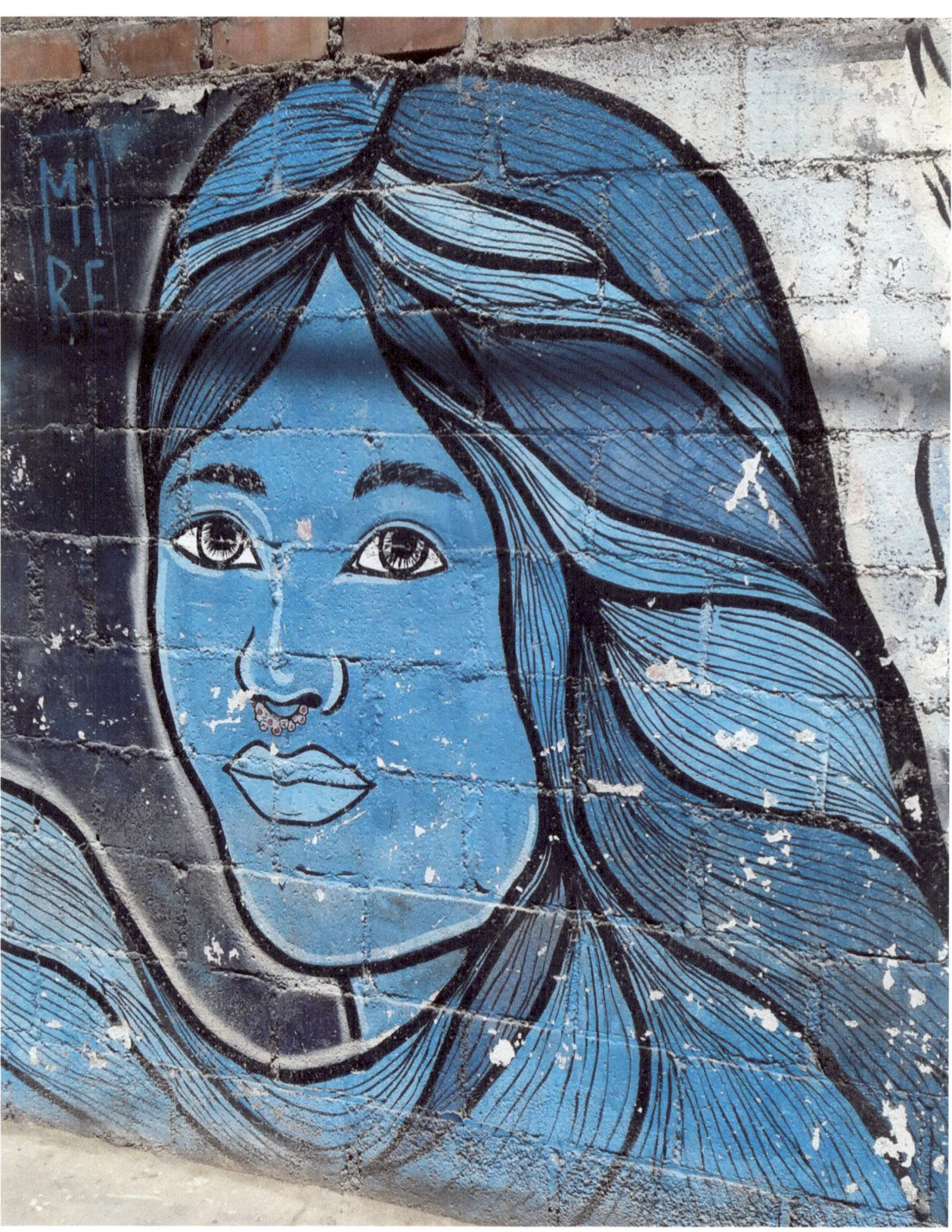

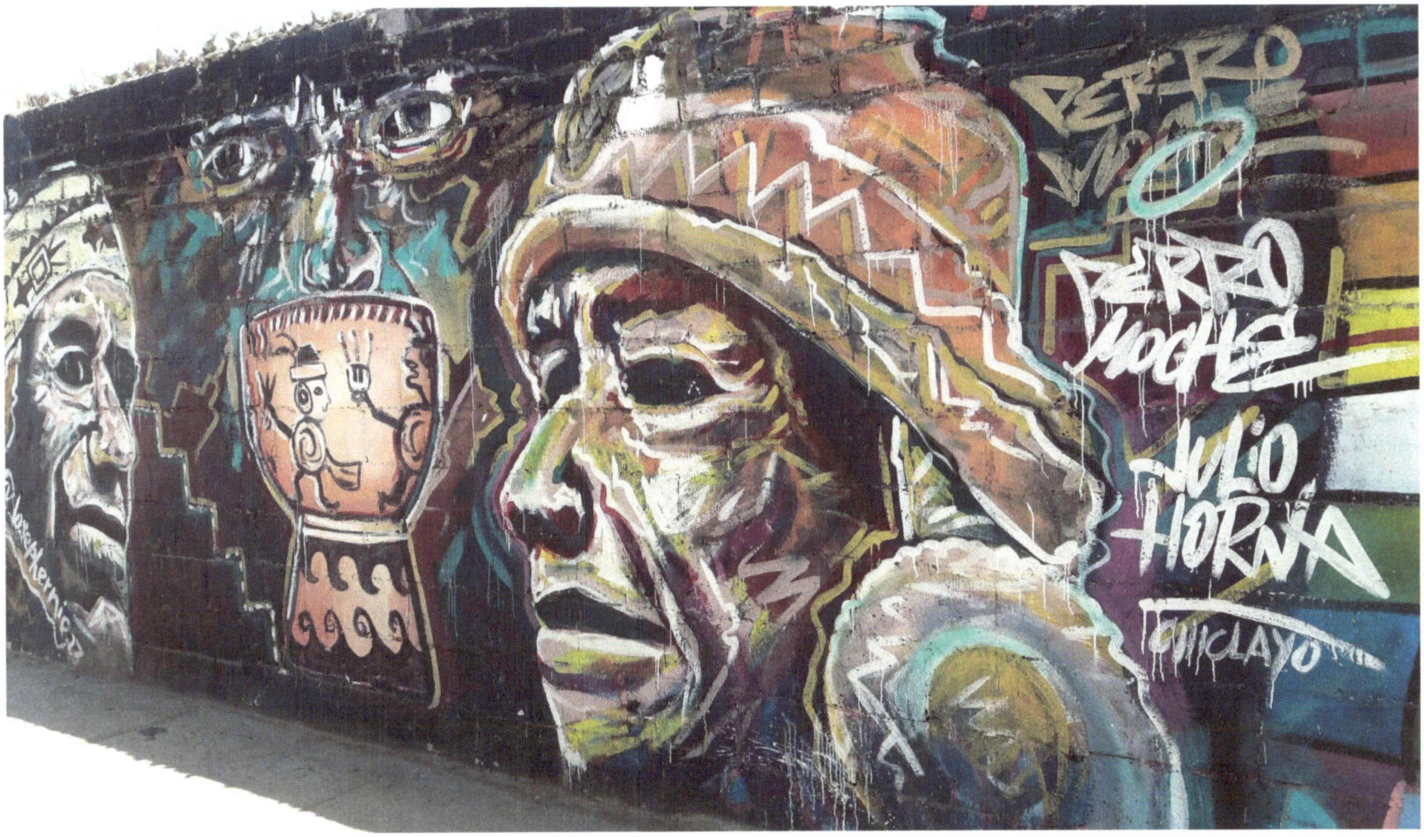
PERRO MOCHE
JULIO HORNA
CHICLAYO

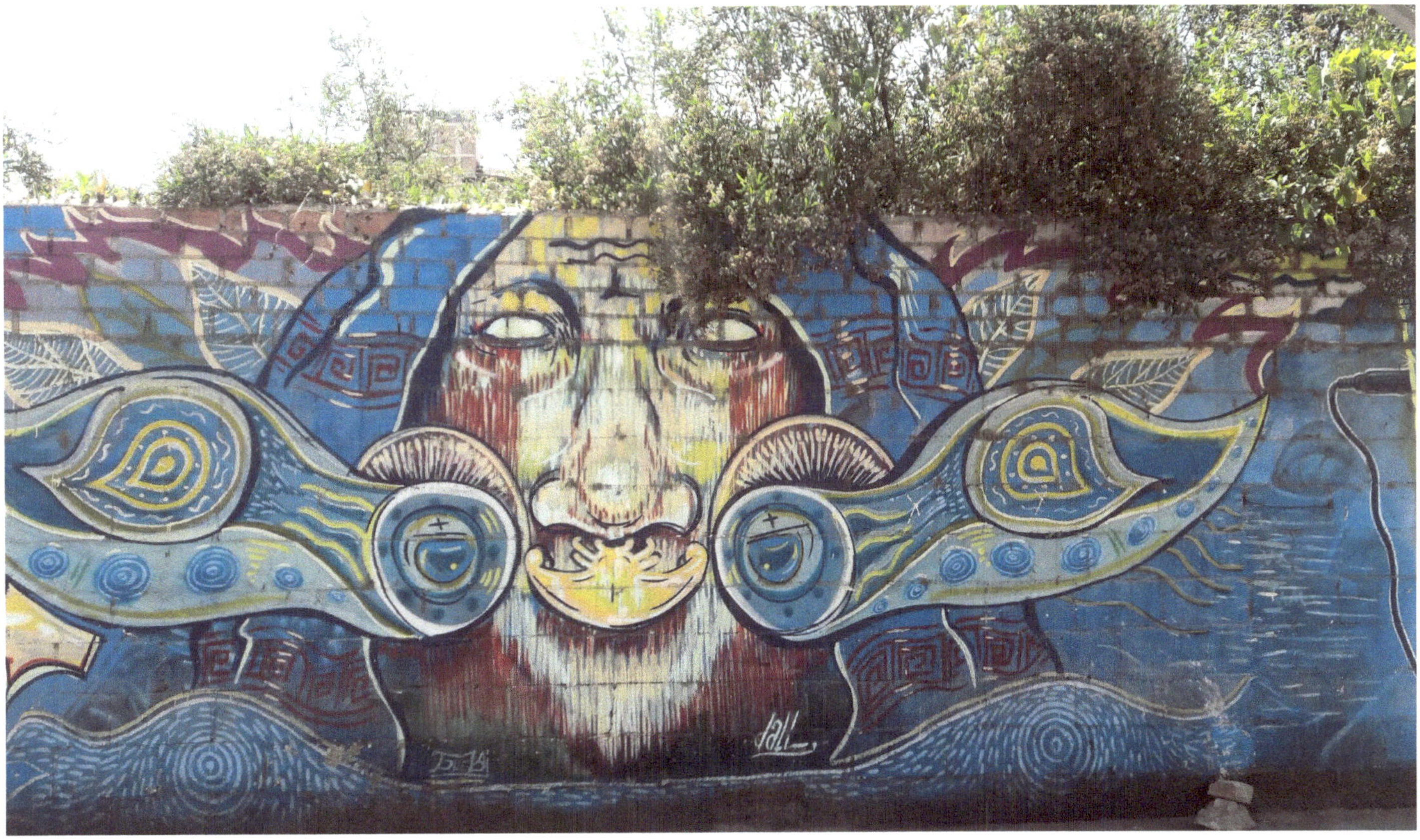

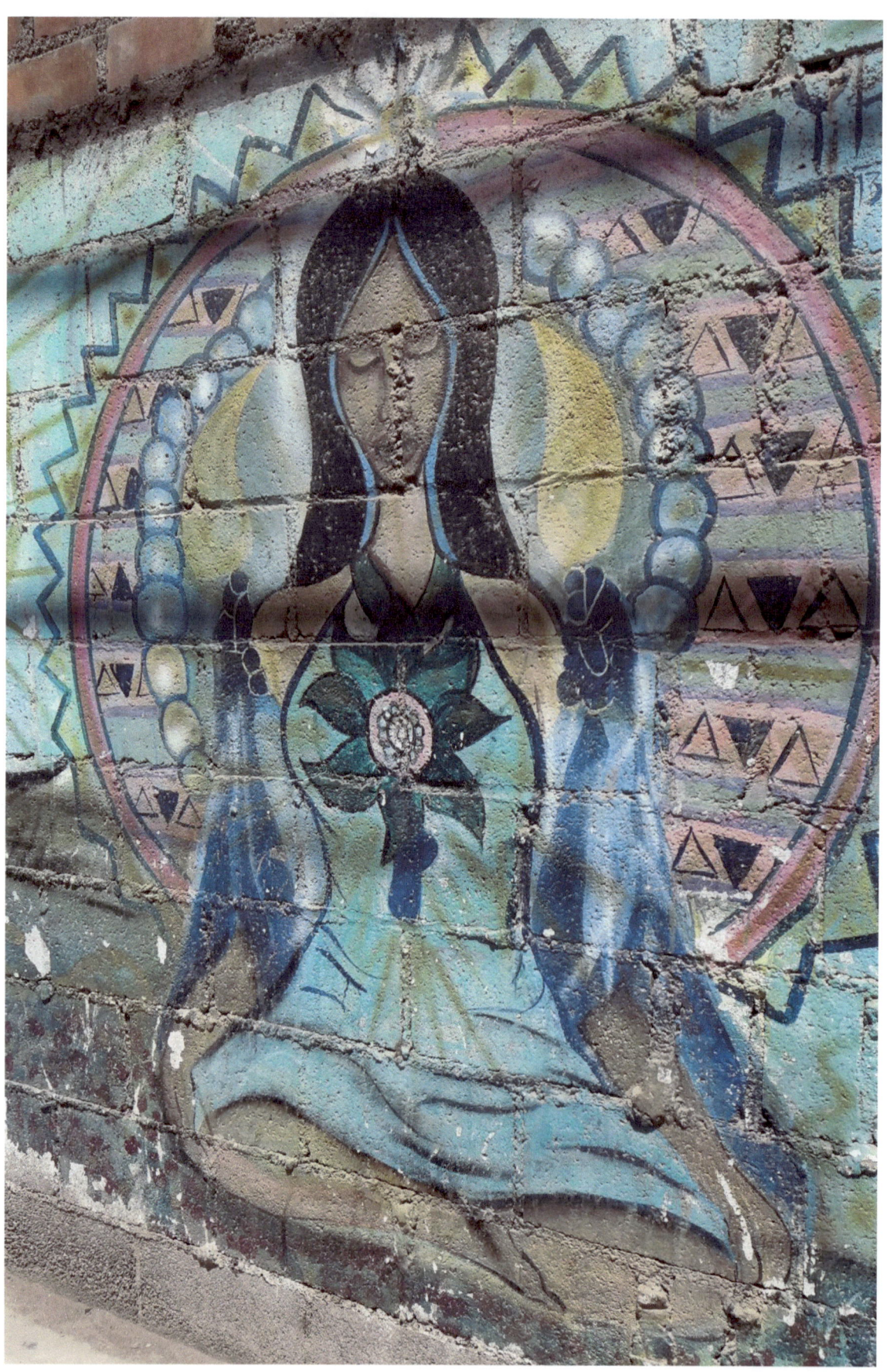

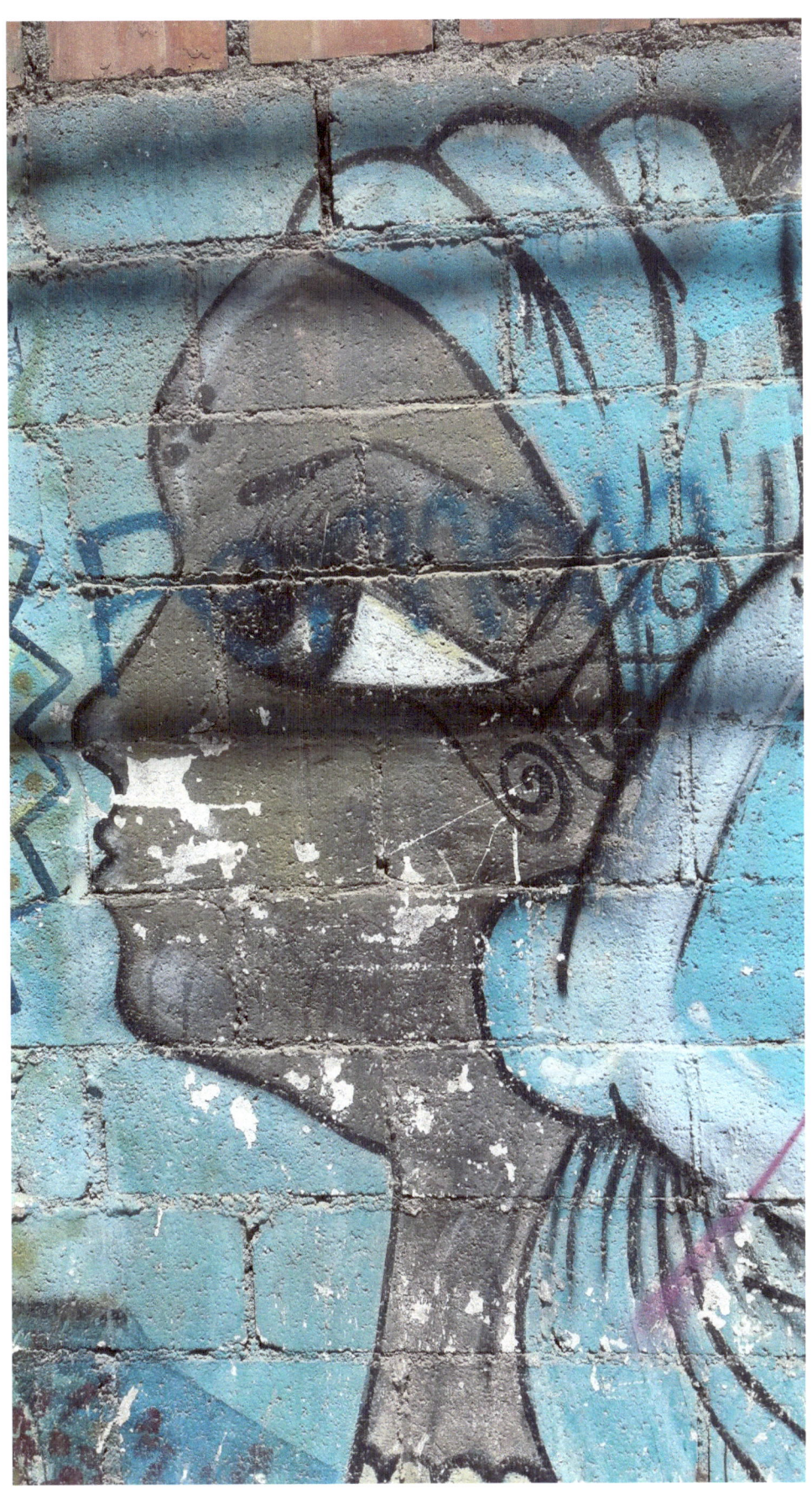

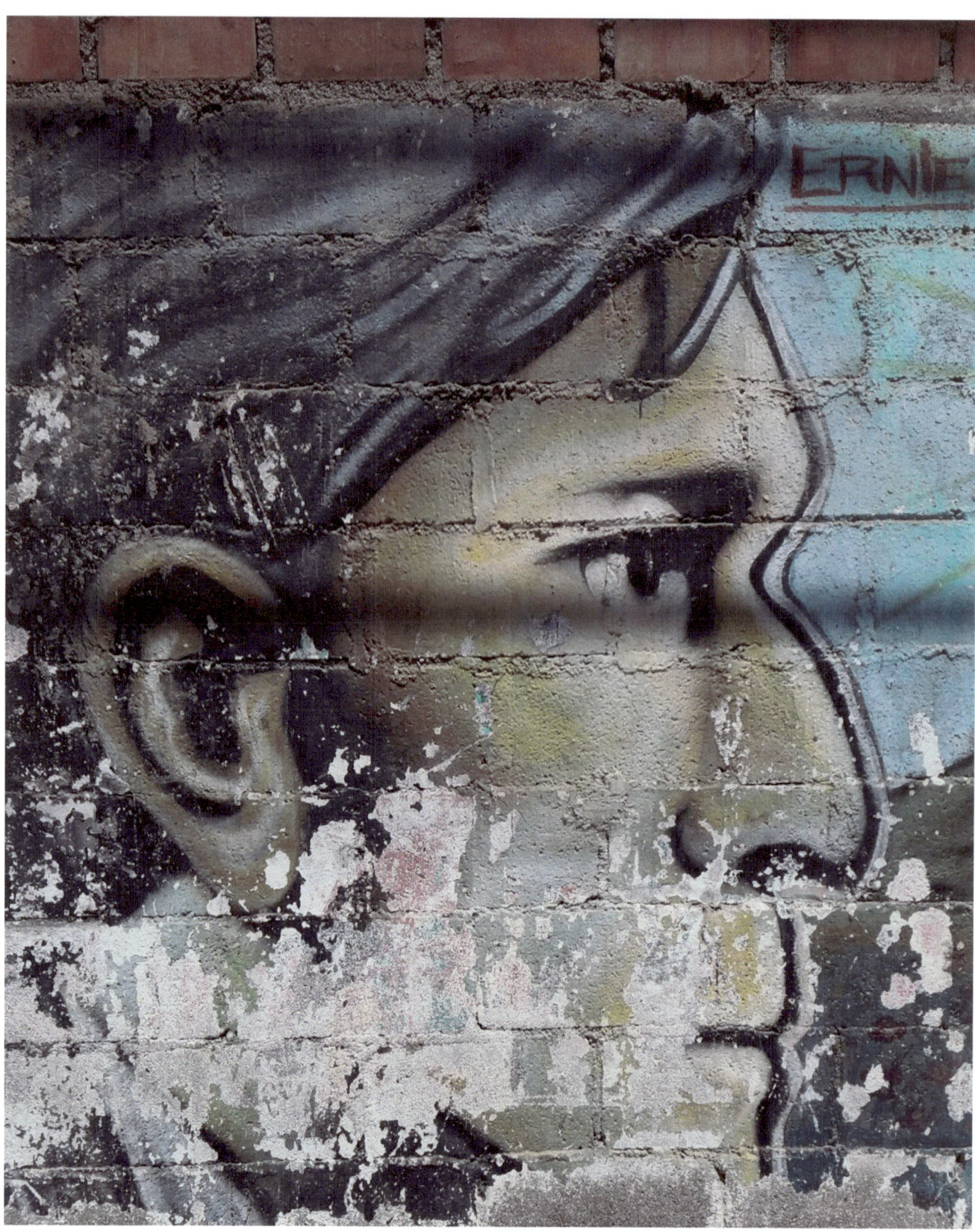

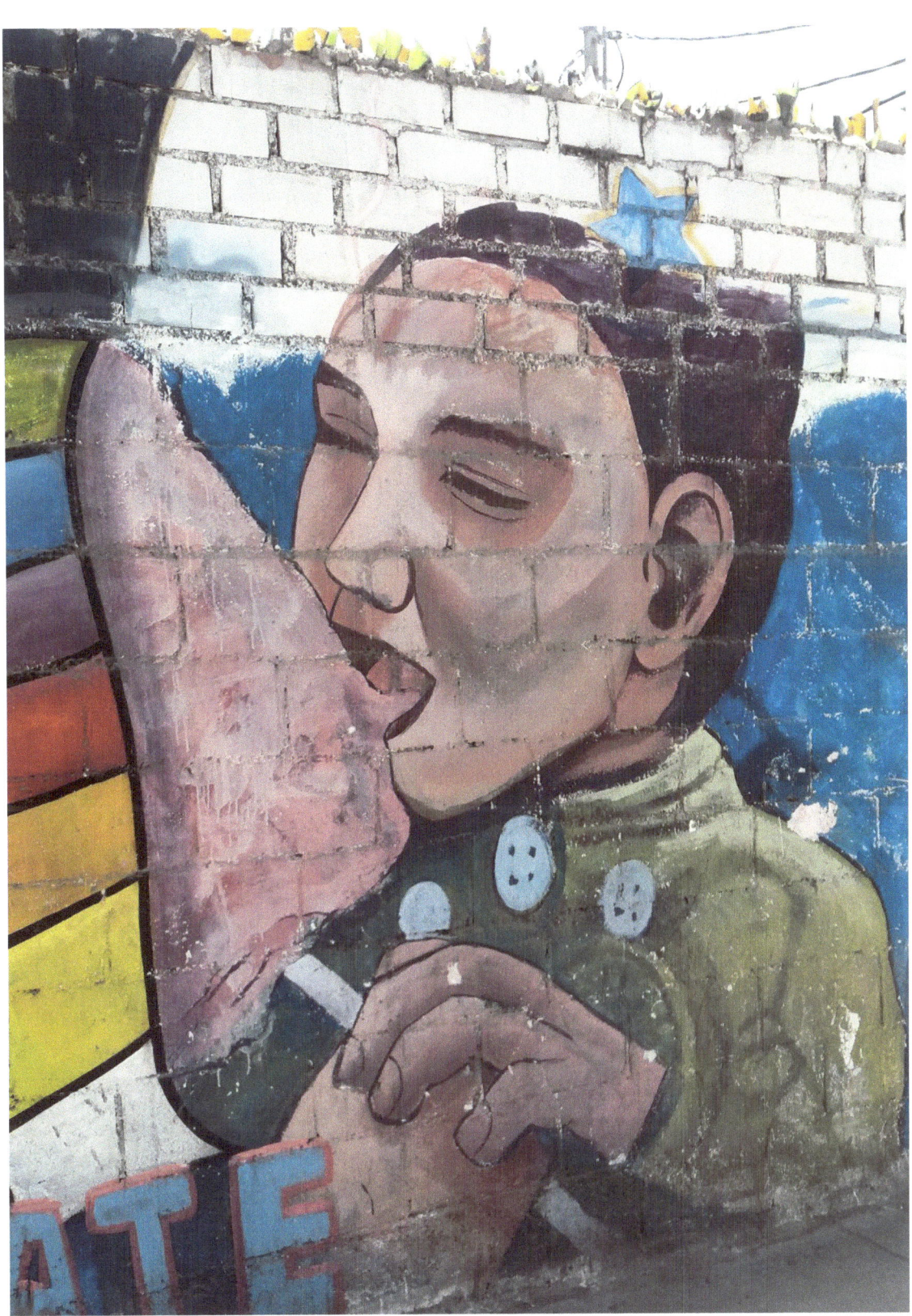

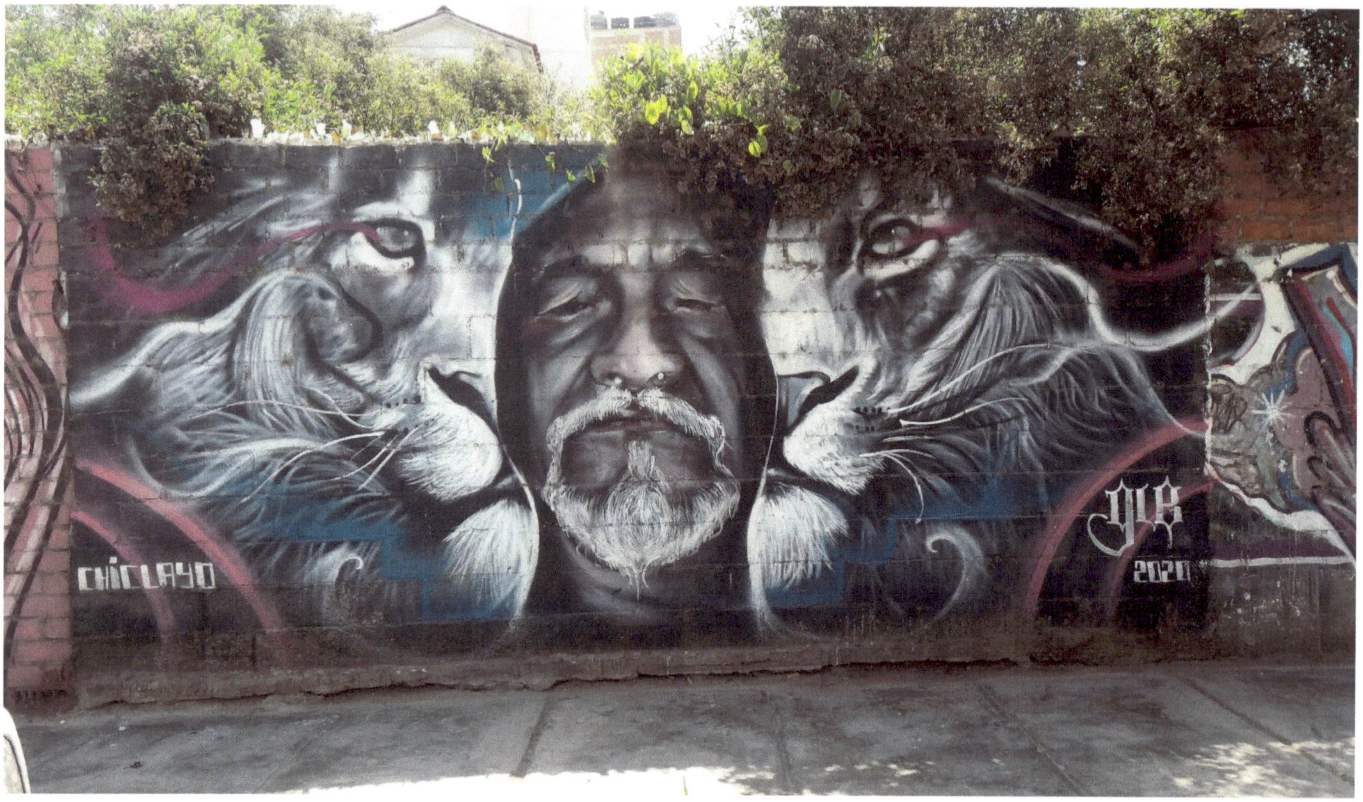

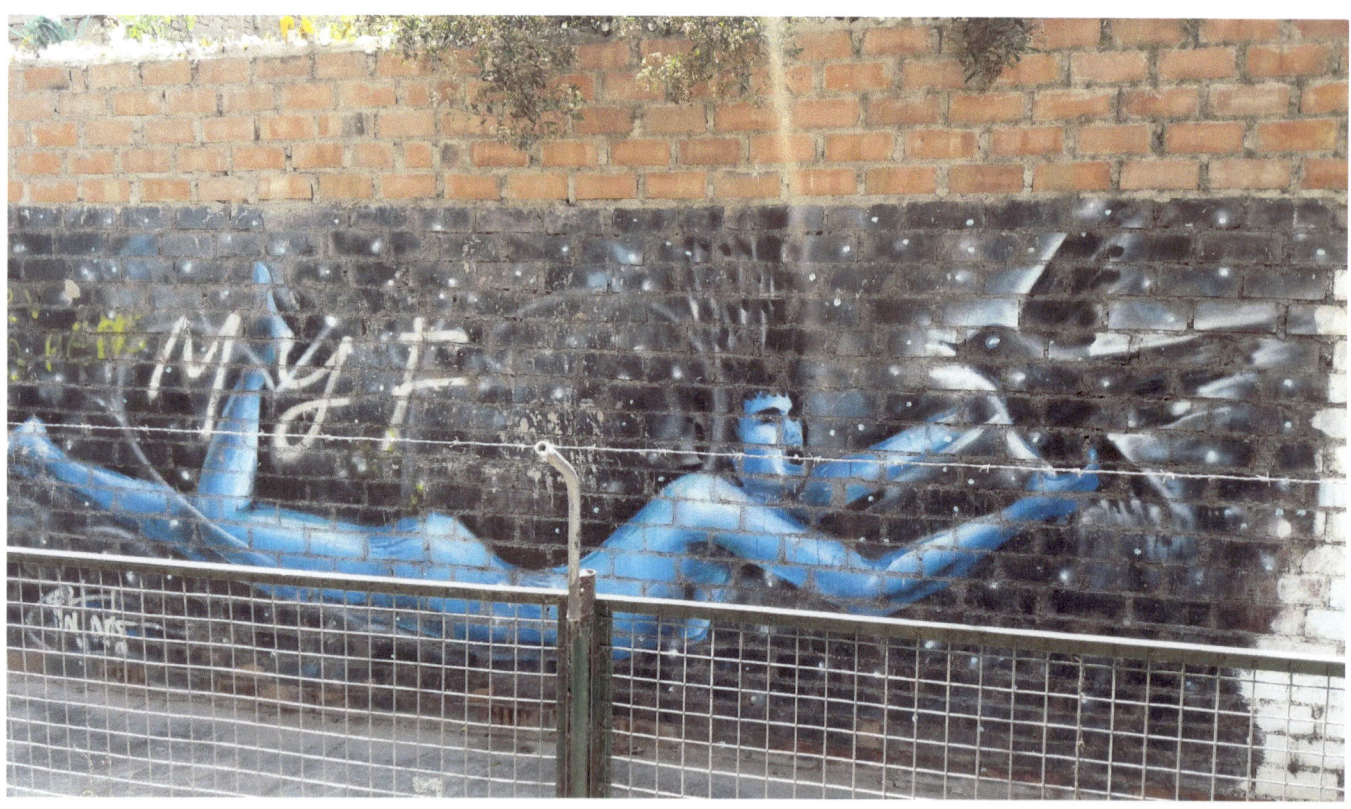

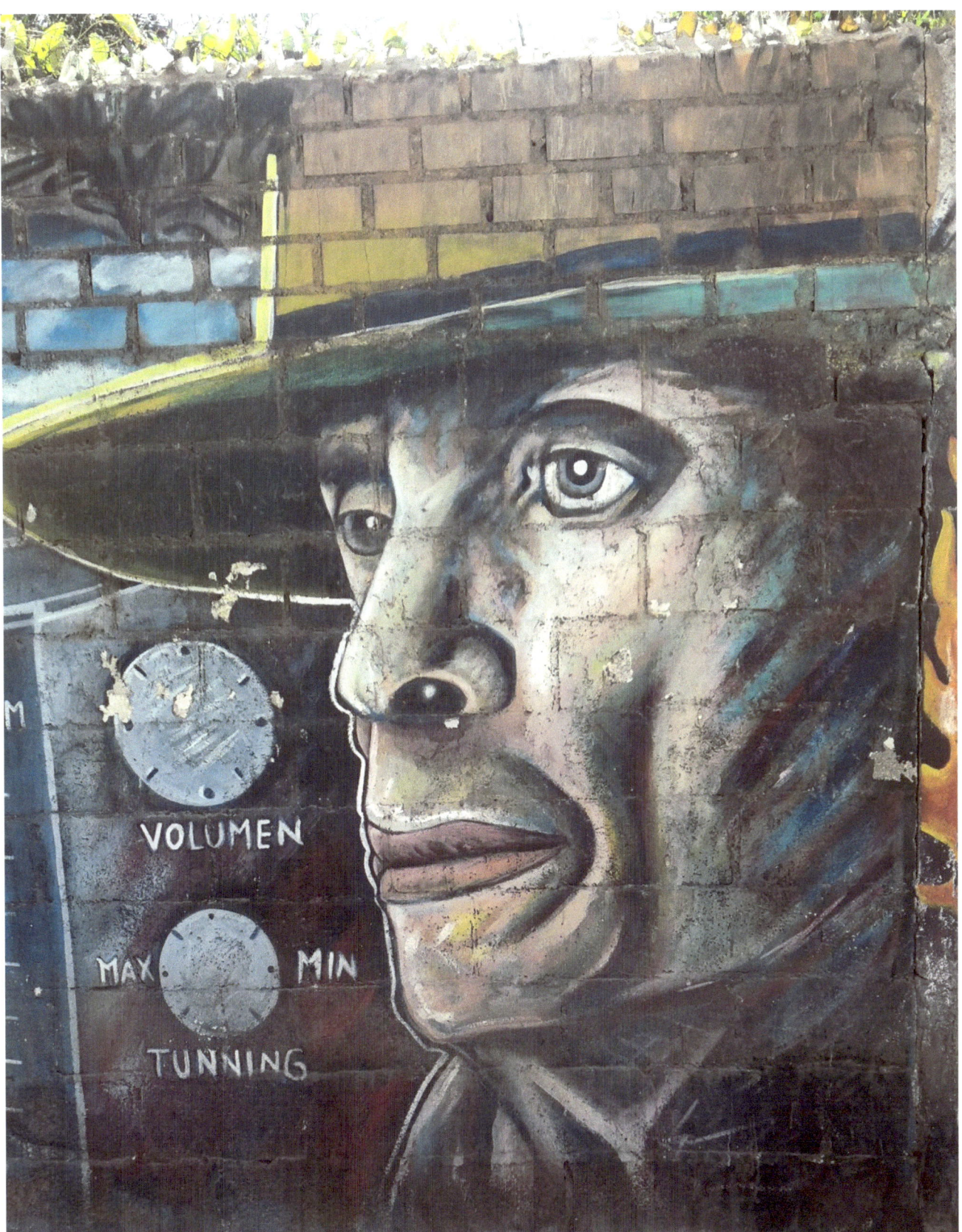

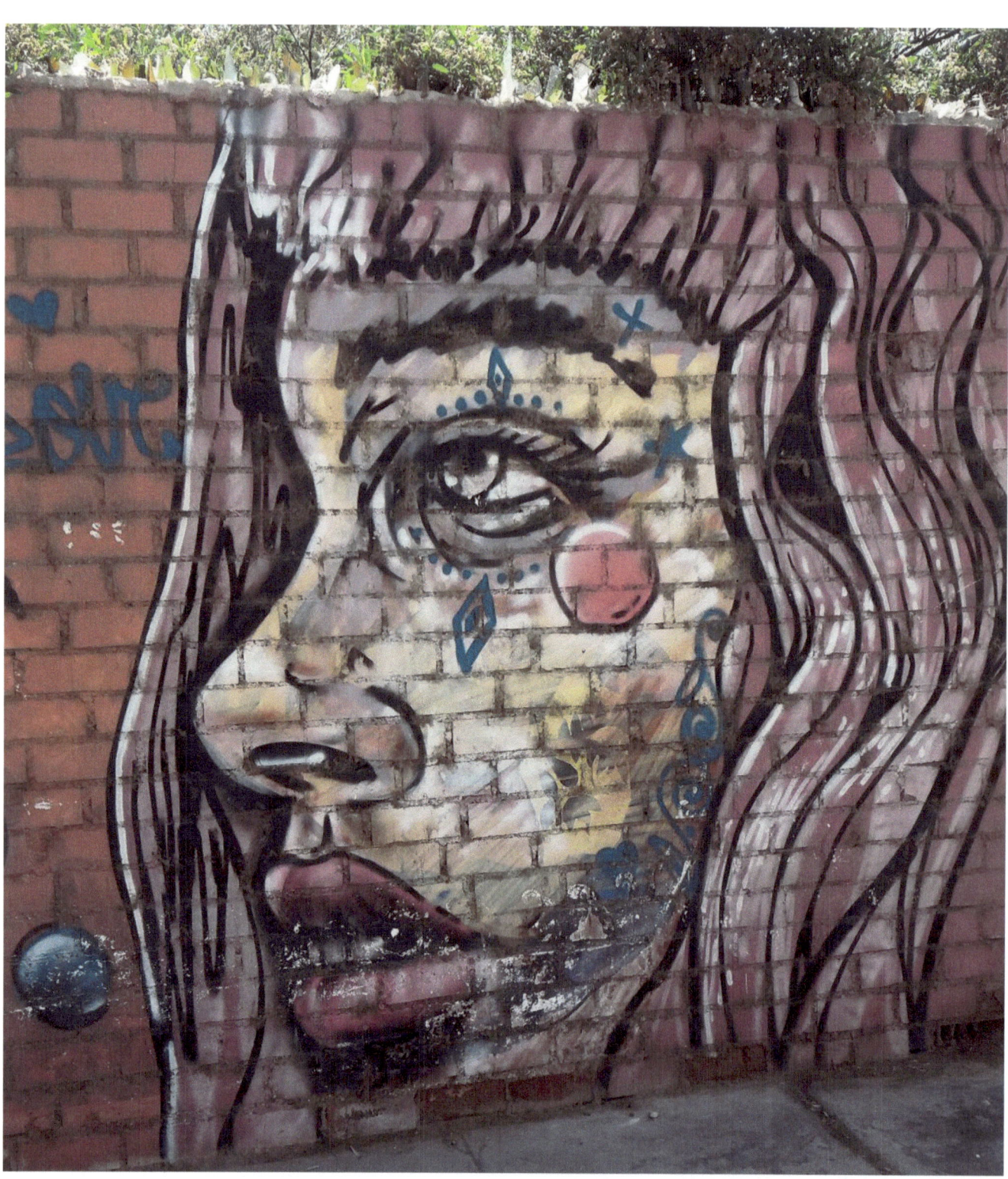

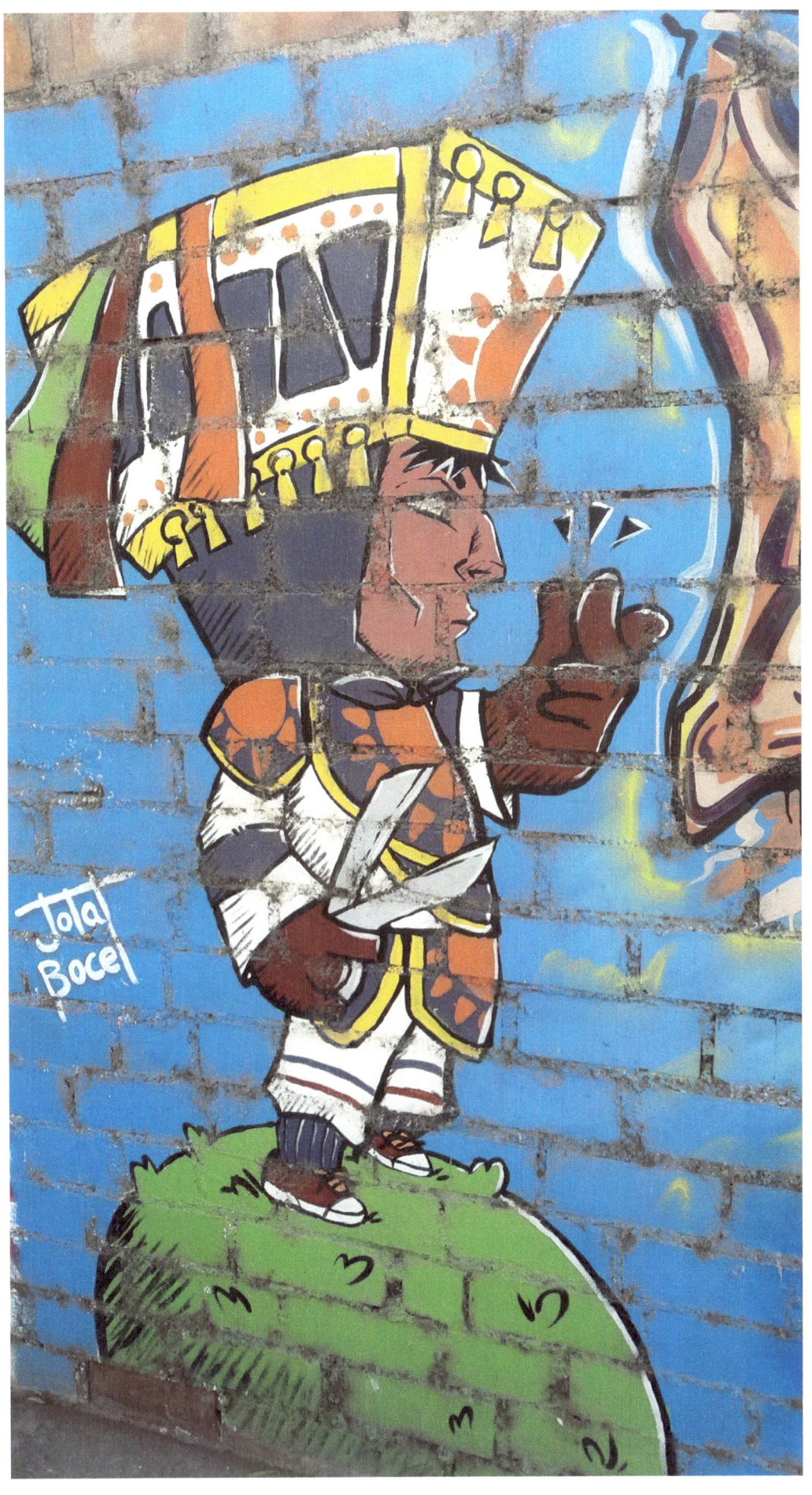

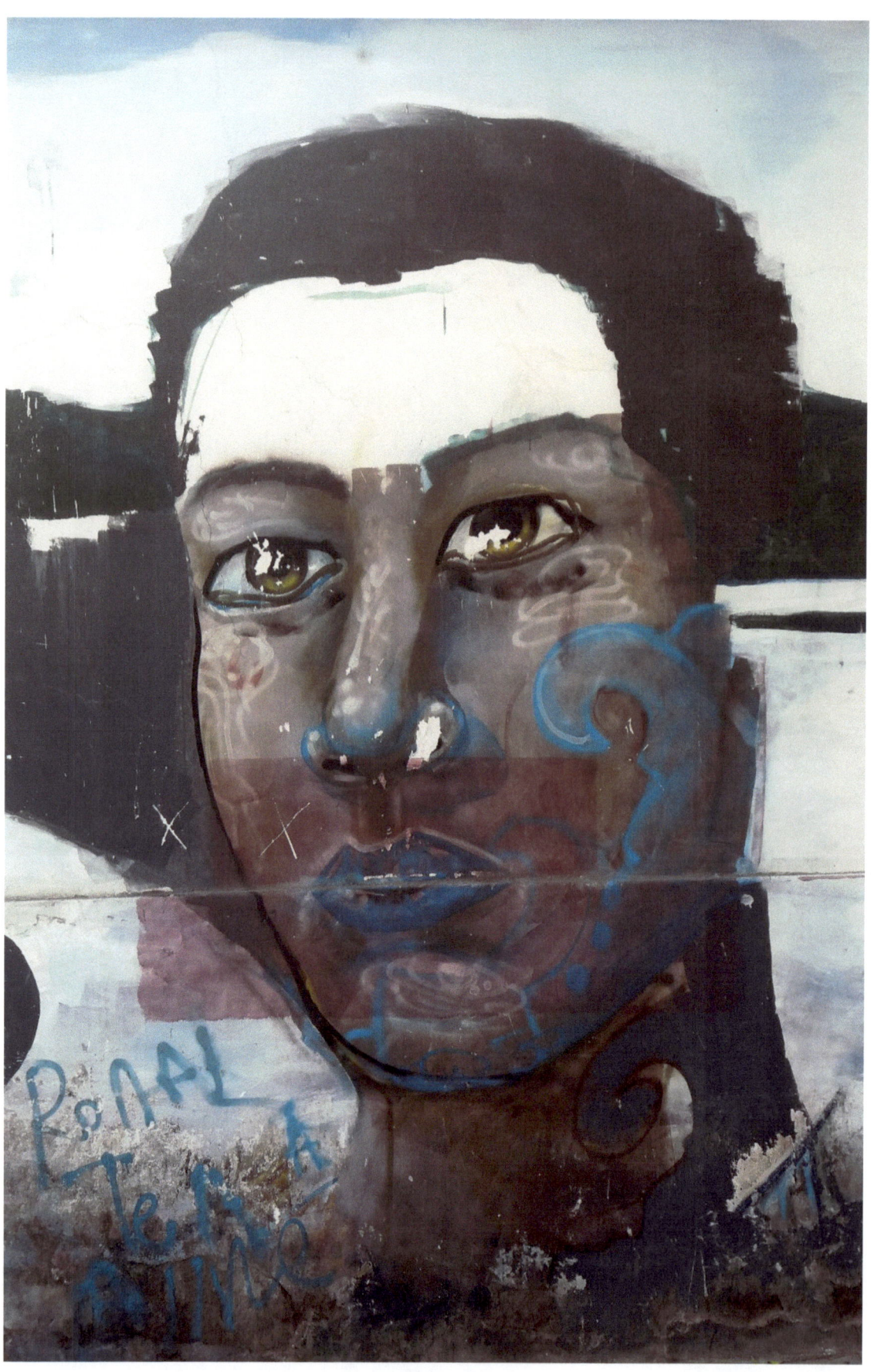

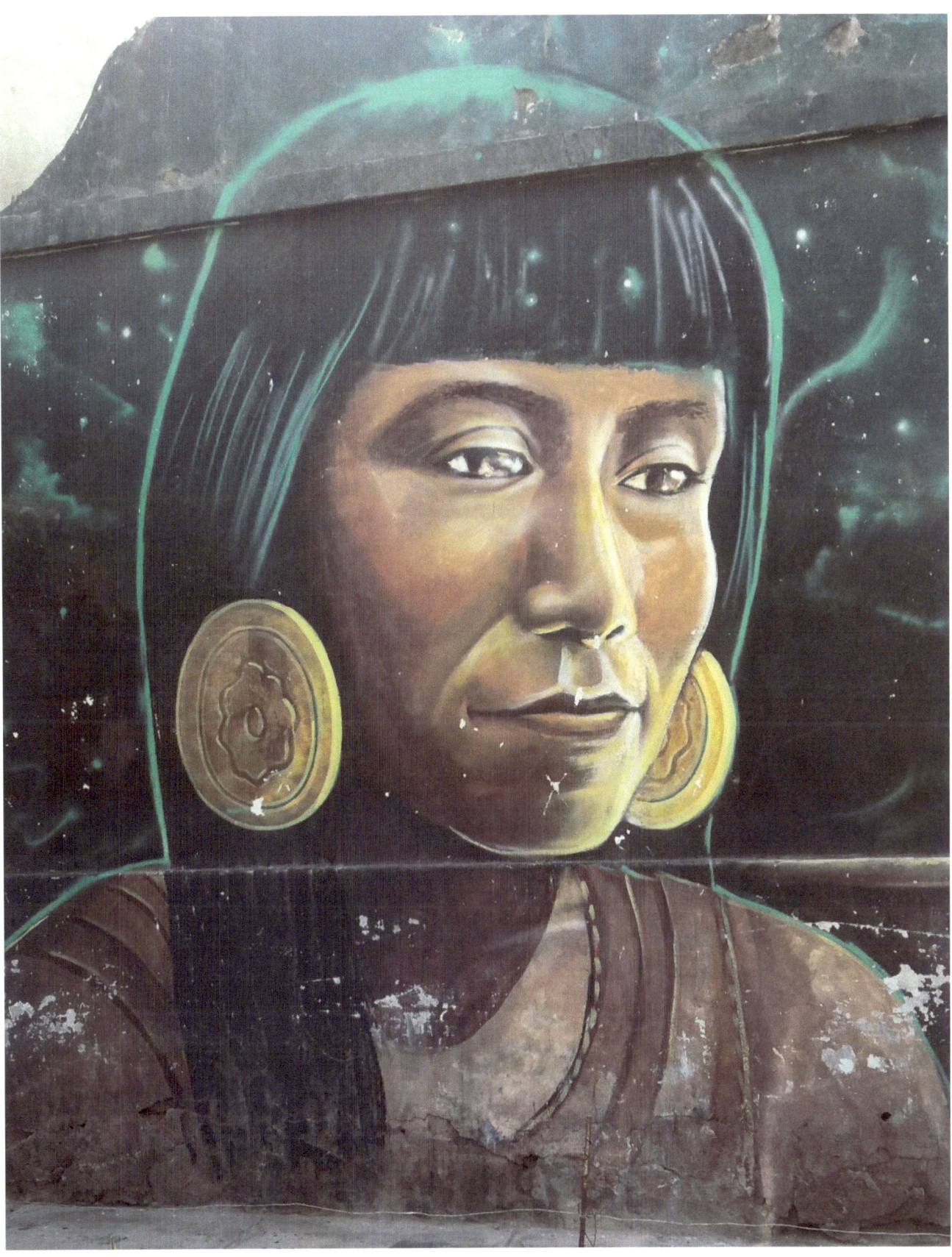

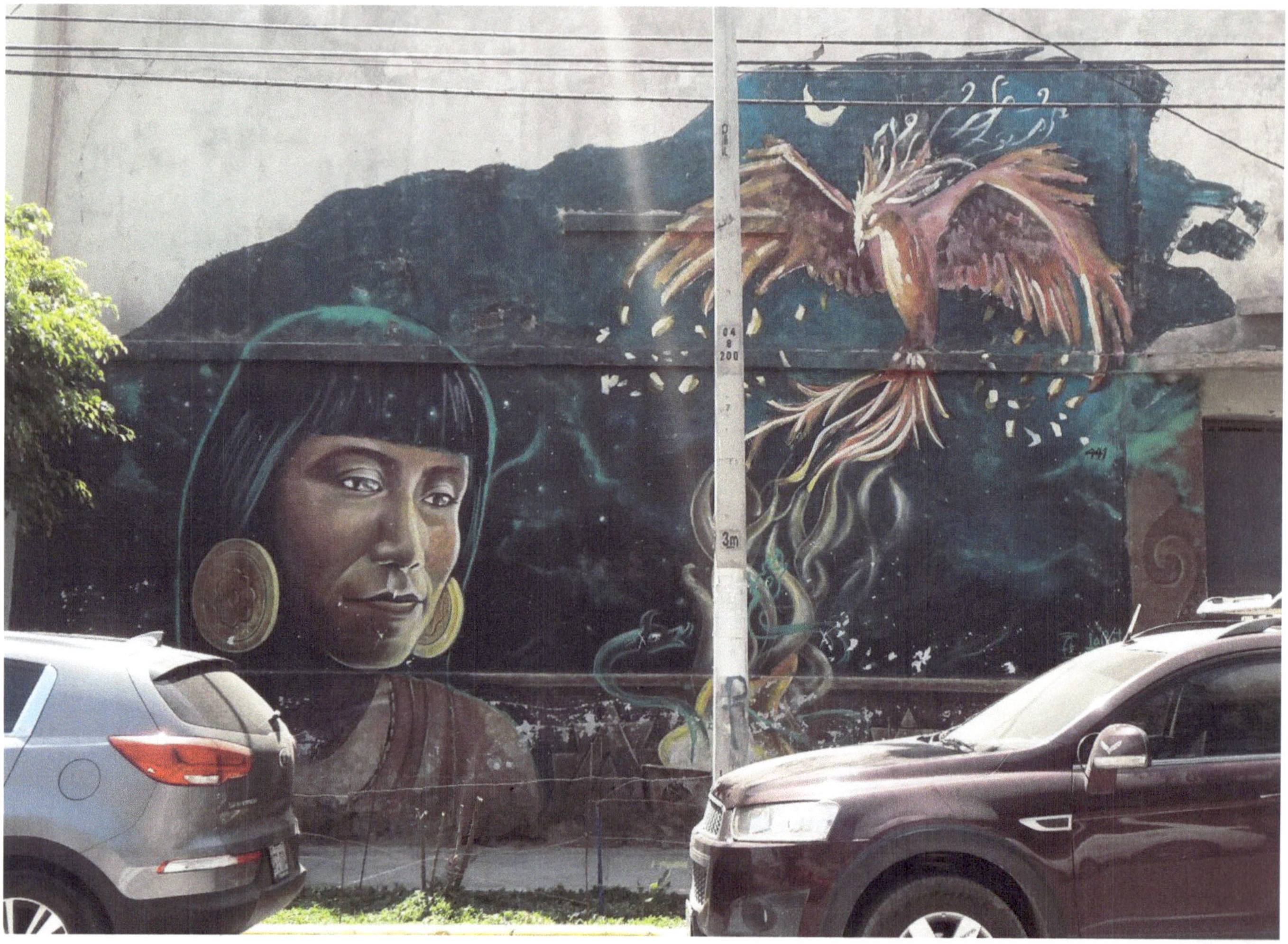

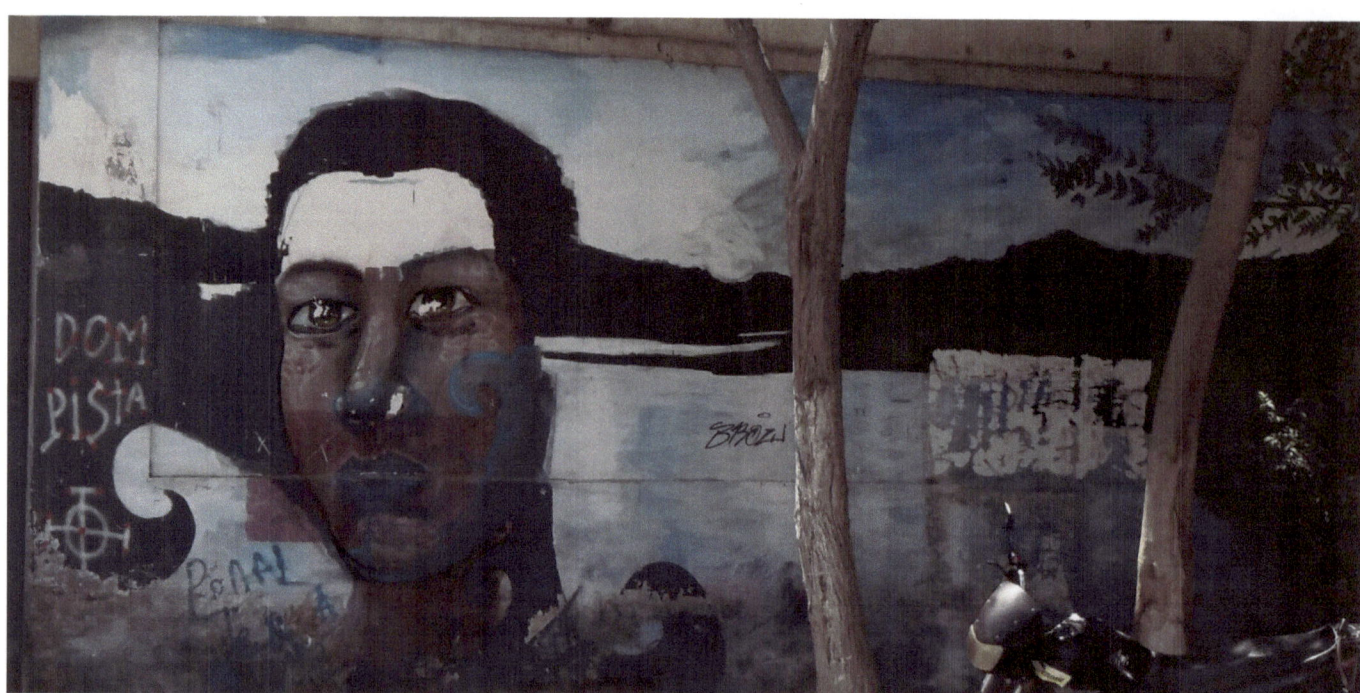

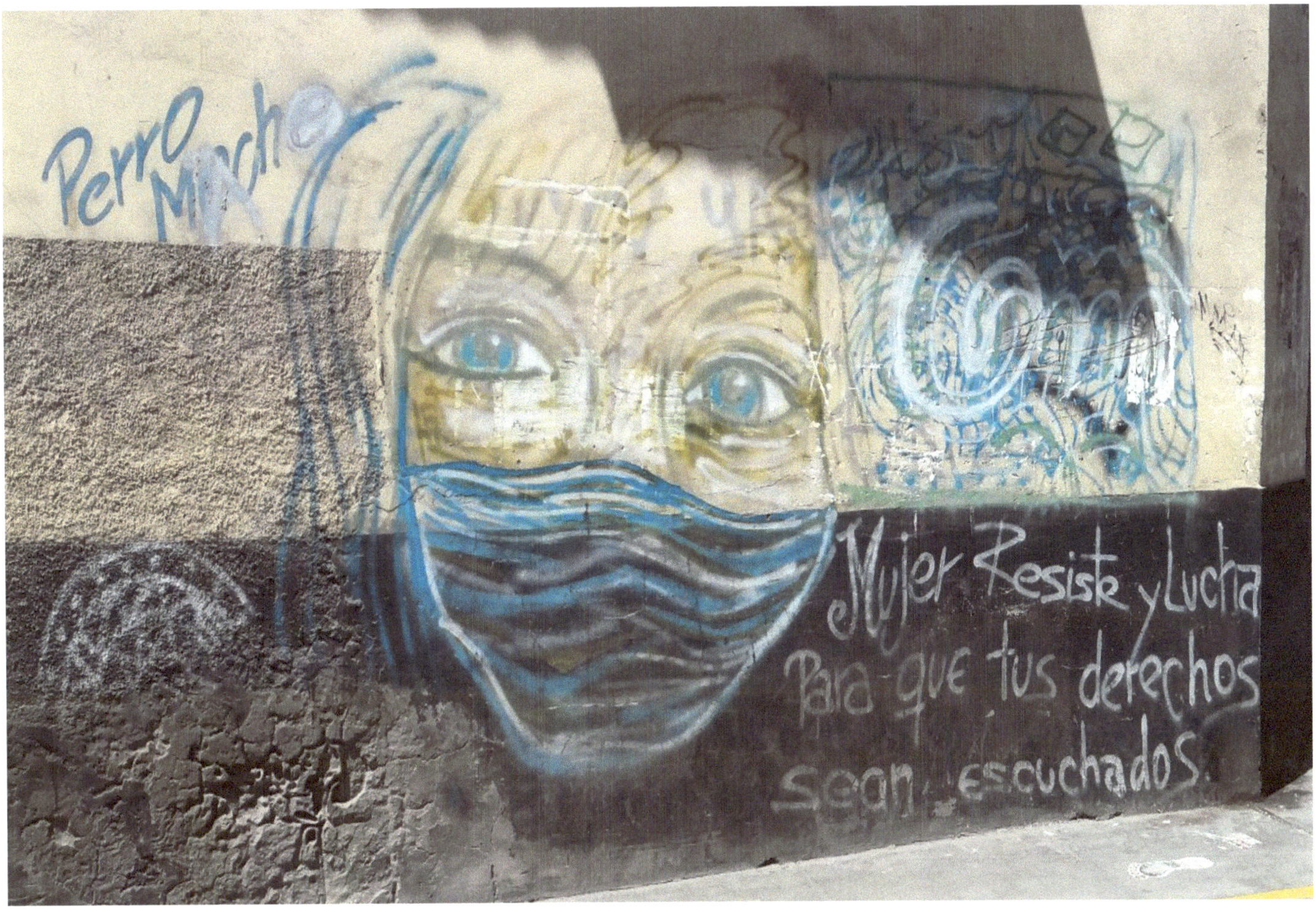

Perro Macho

Mujer Resiste y Lucha
Para que tus derechos
sean escuchados

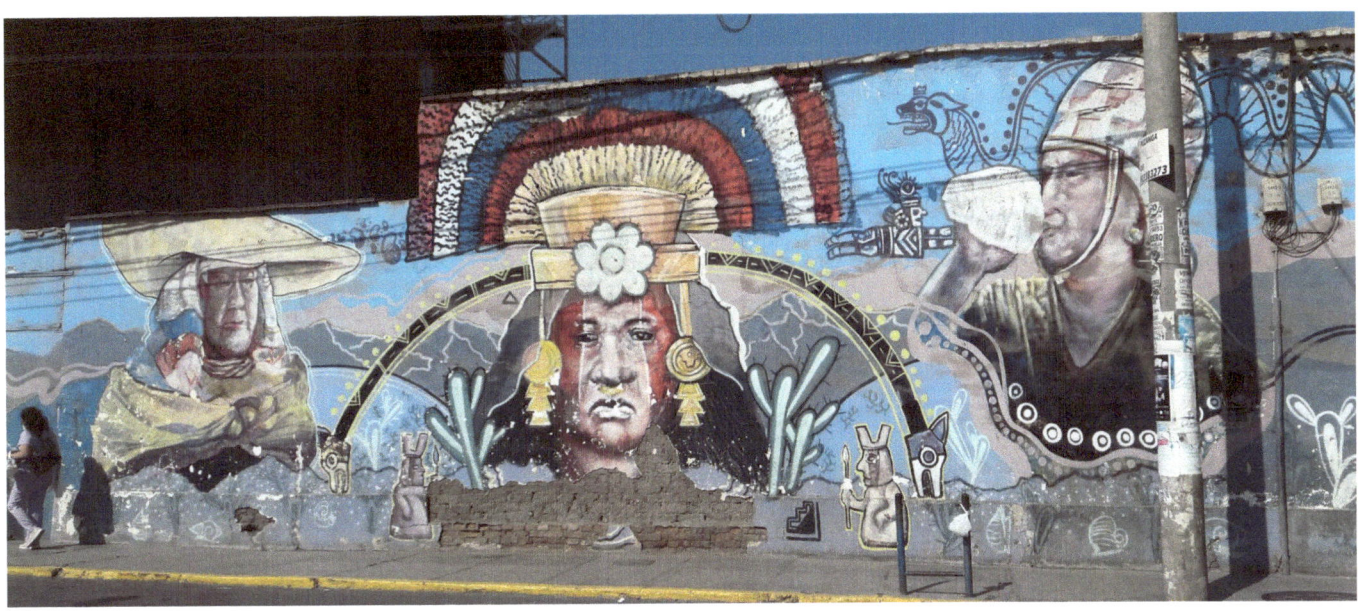

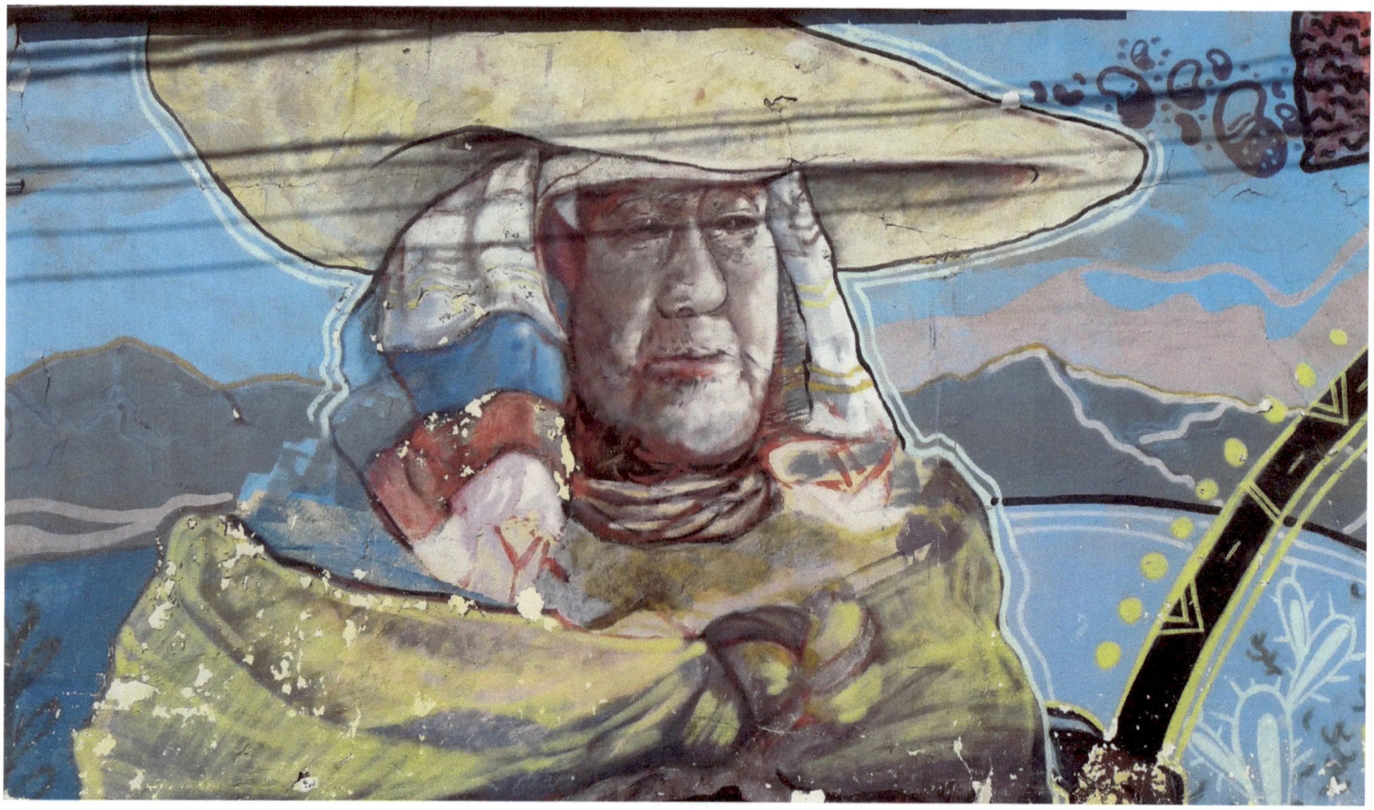

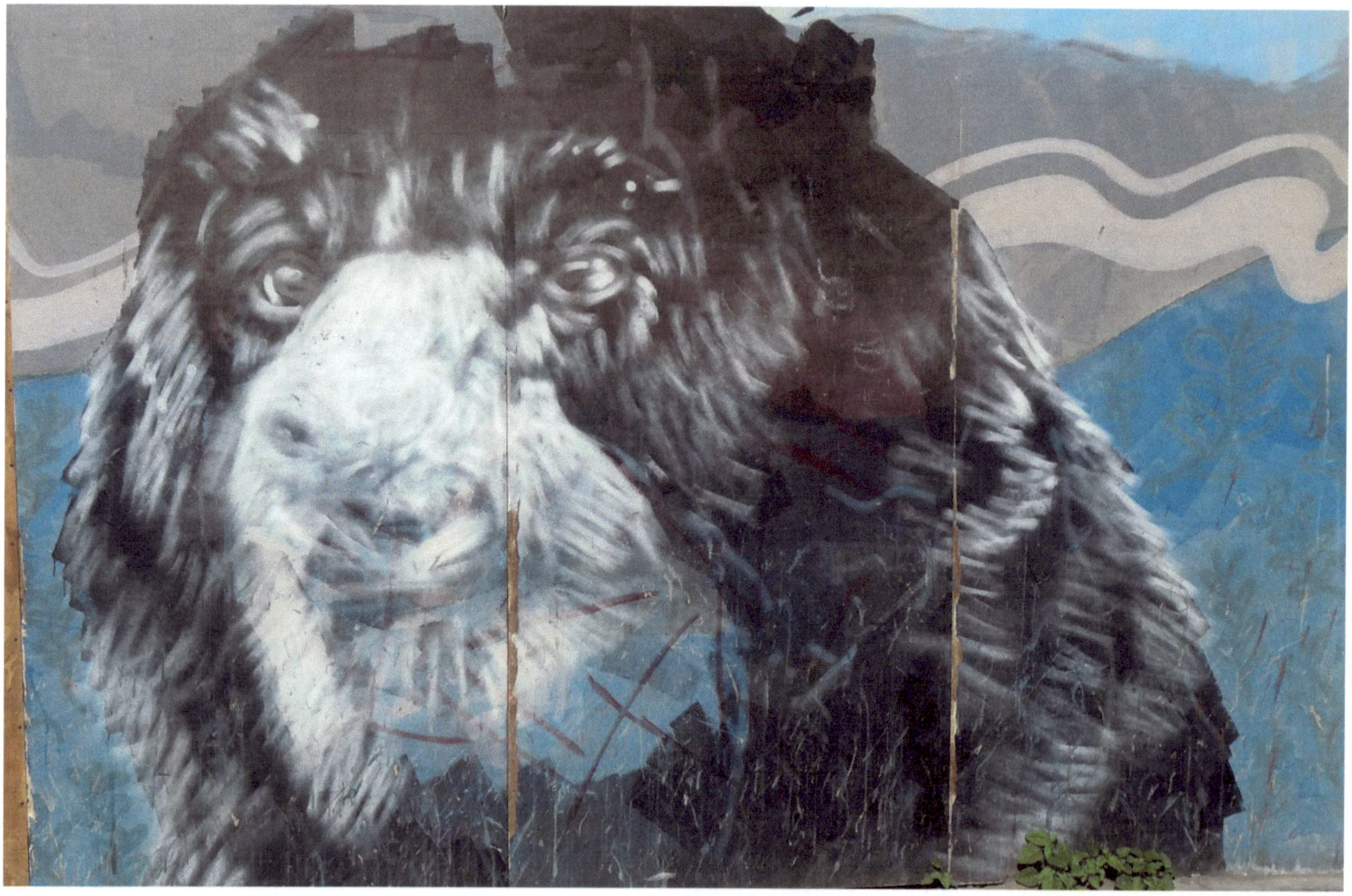

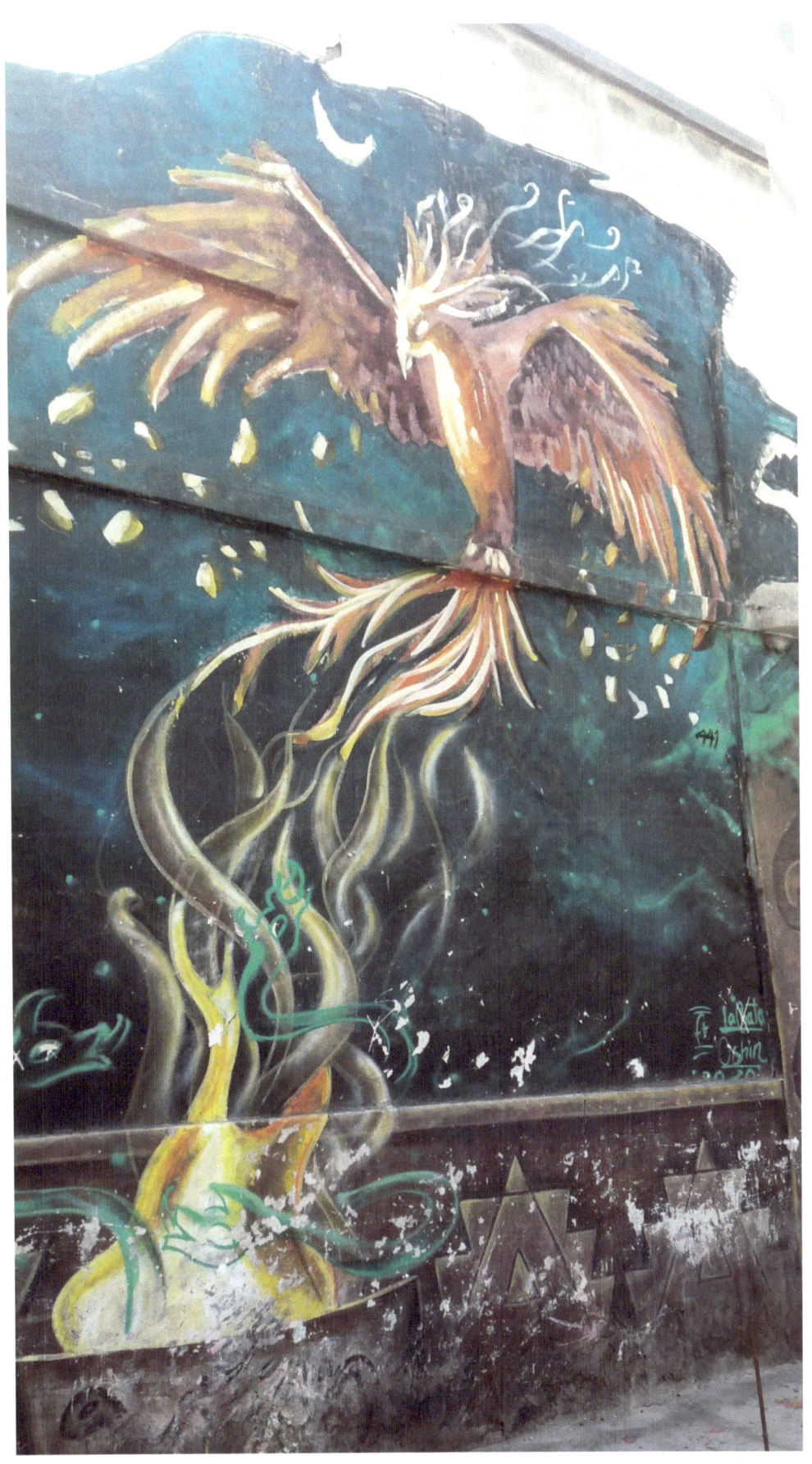

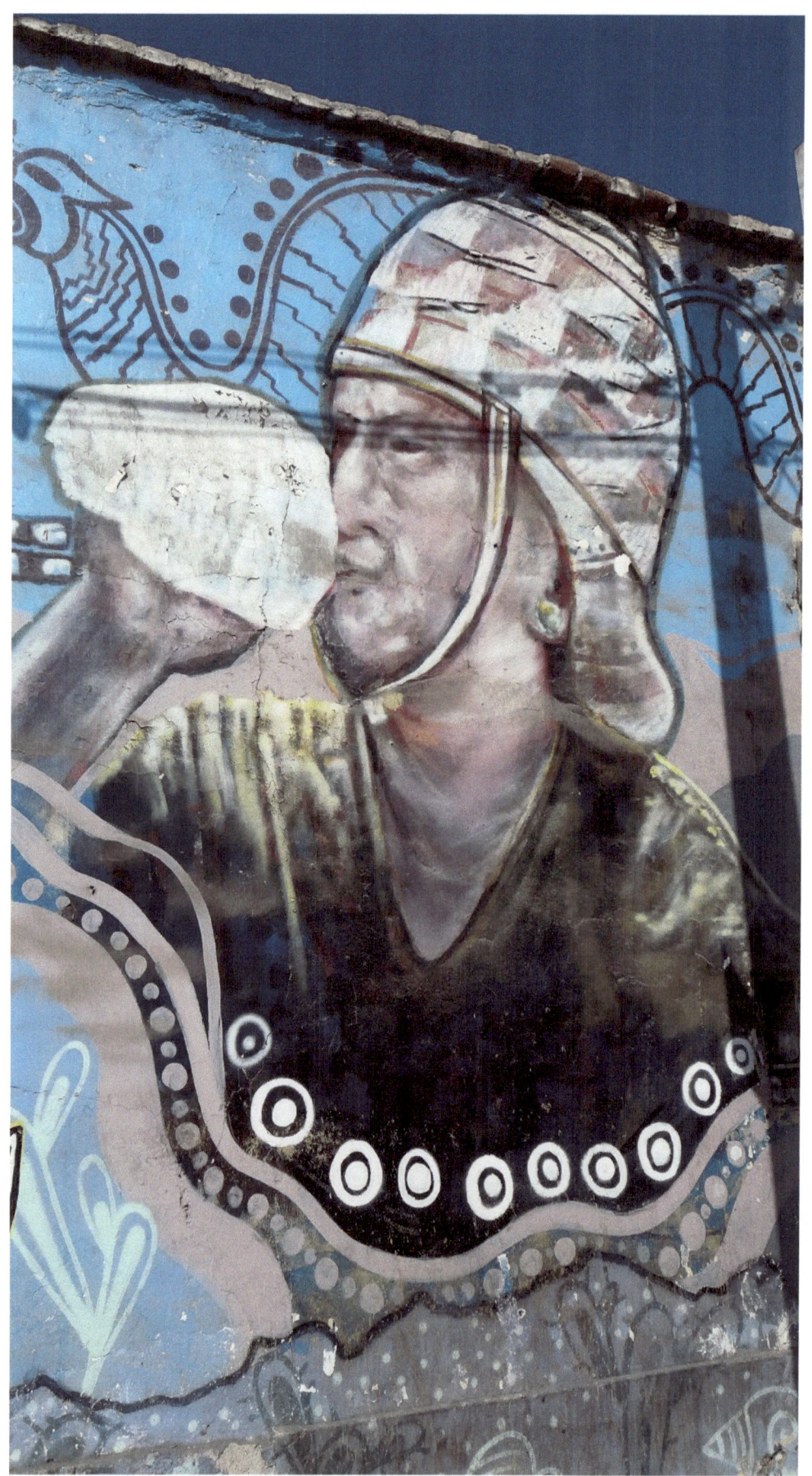

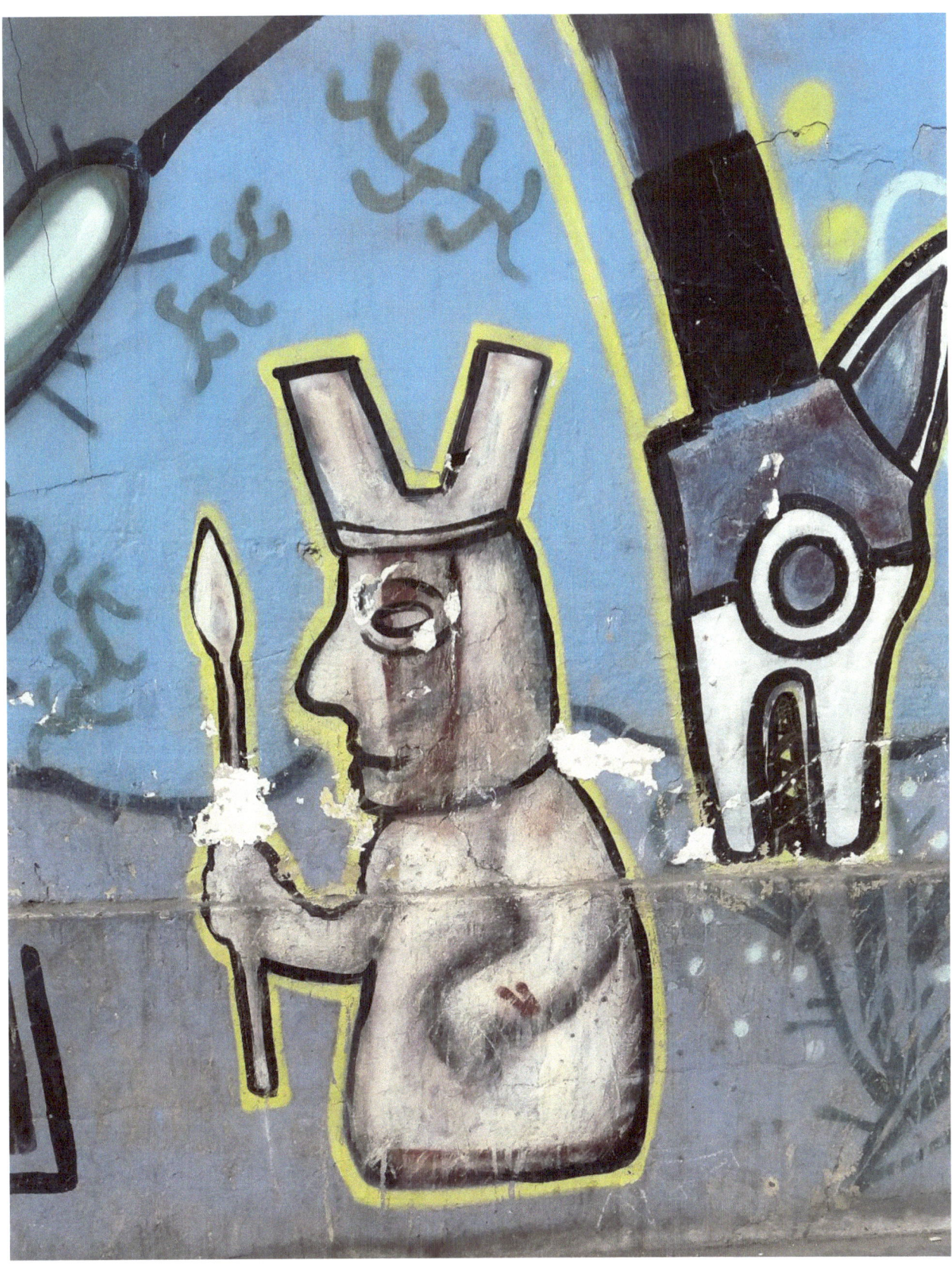

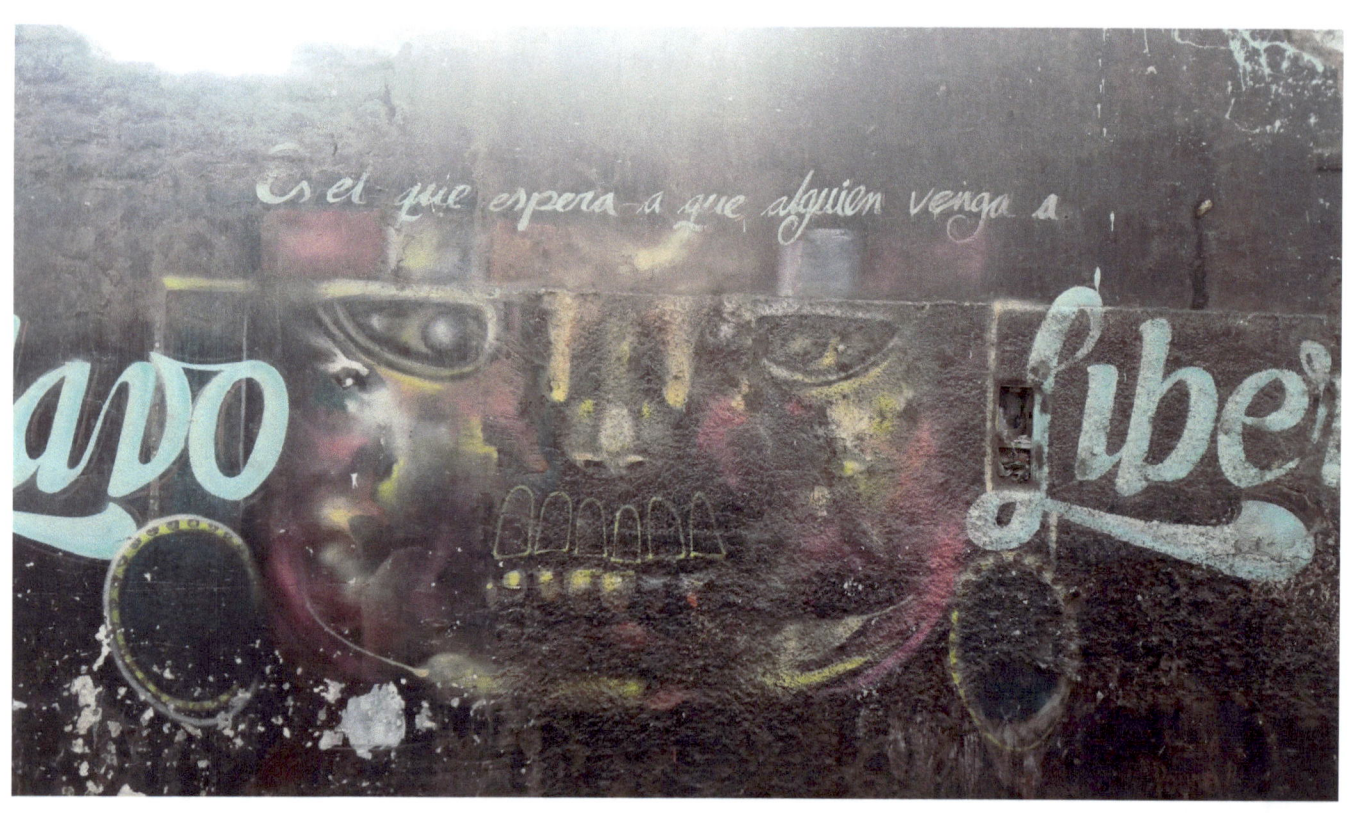

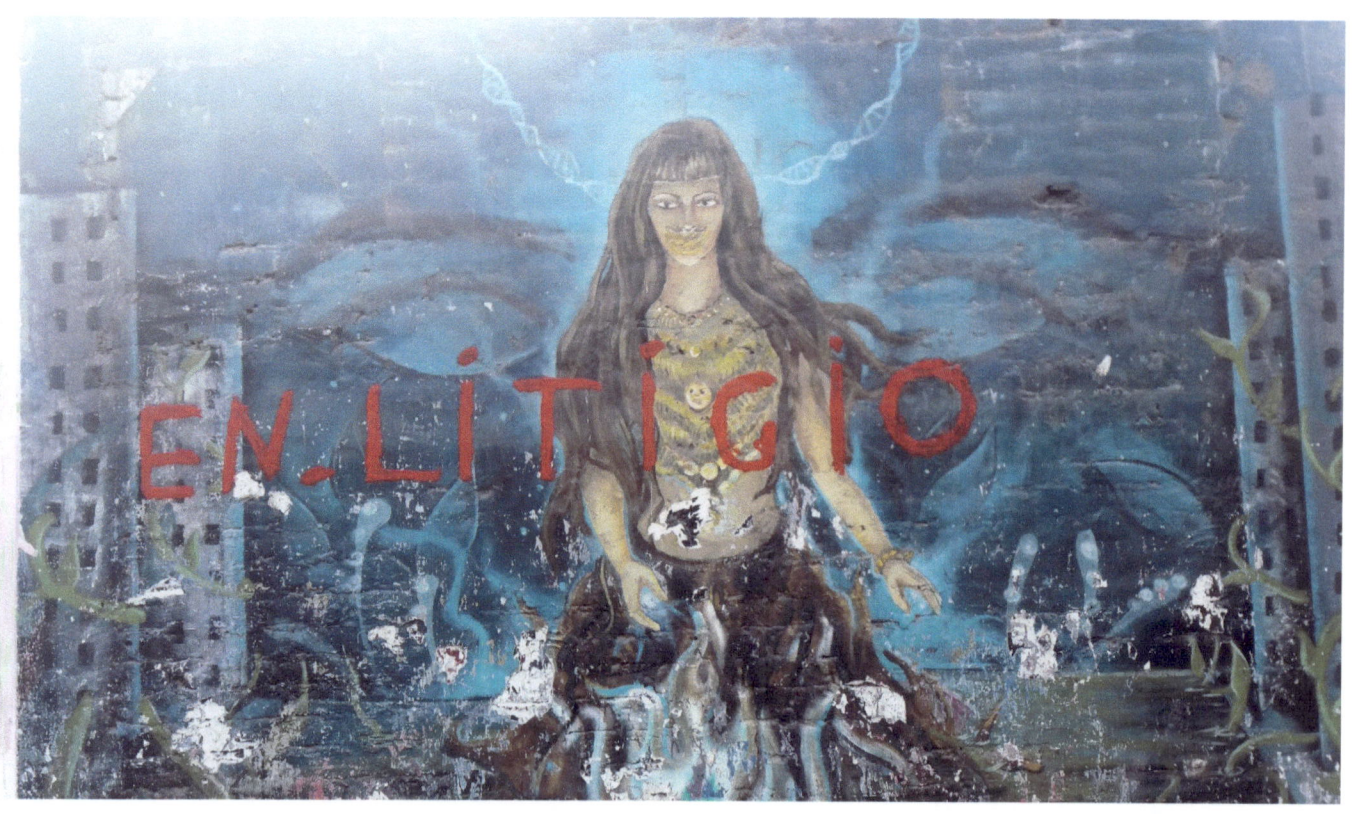

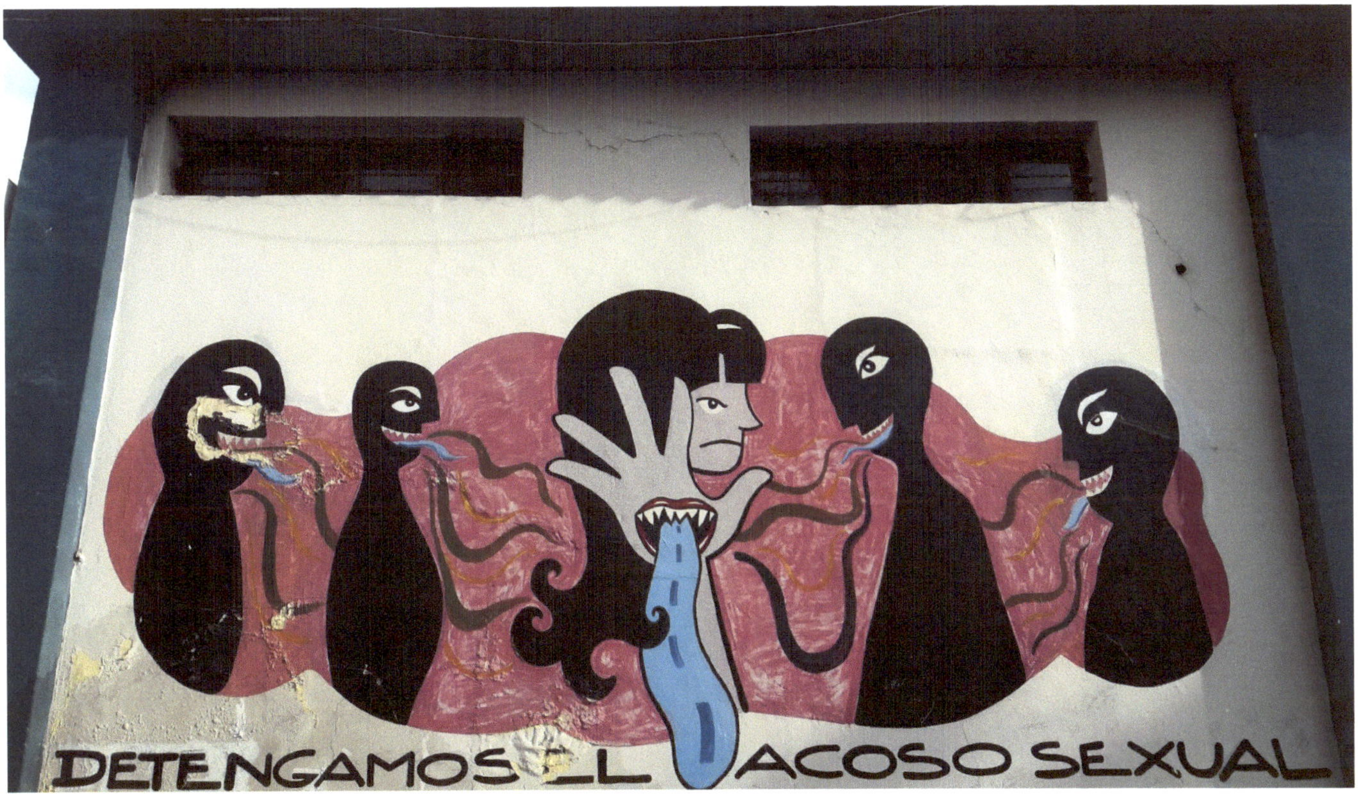

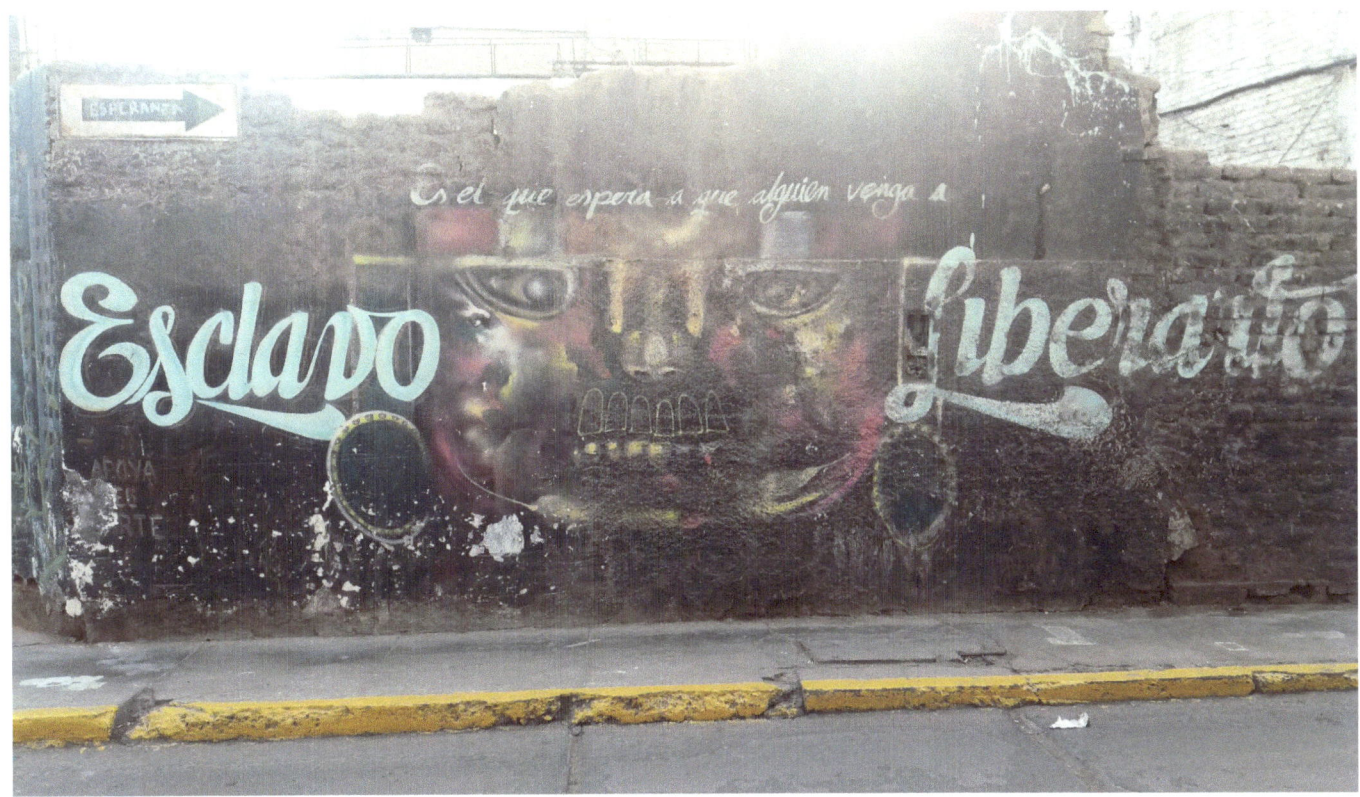

DETENGAMOS EL ACOSO SEXUAL

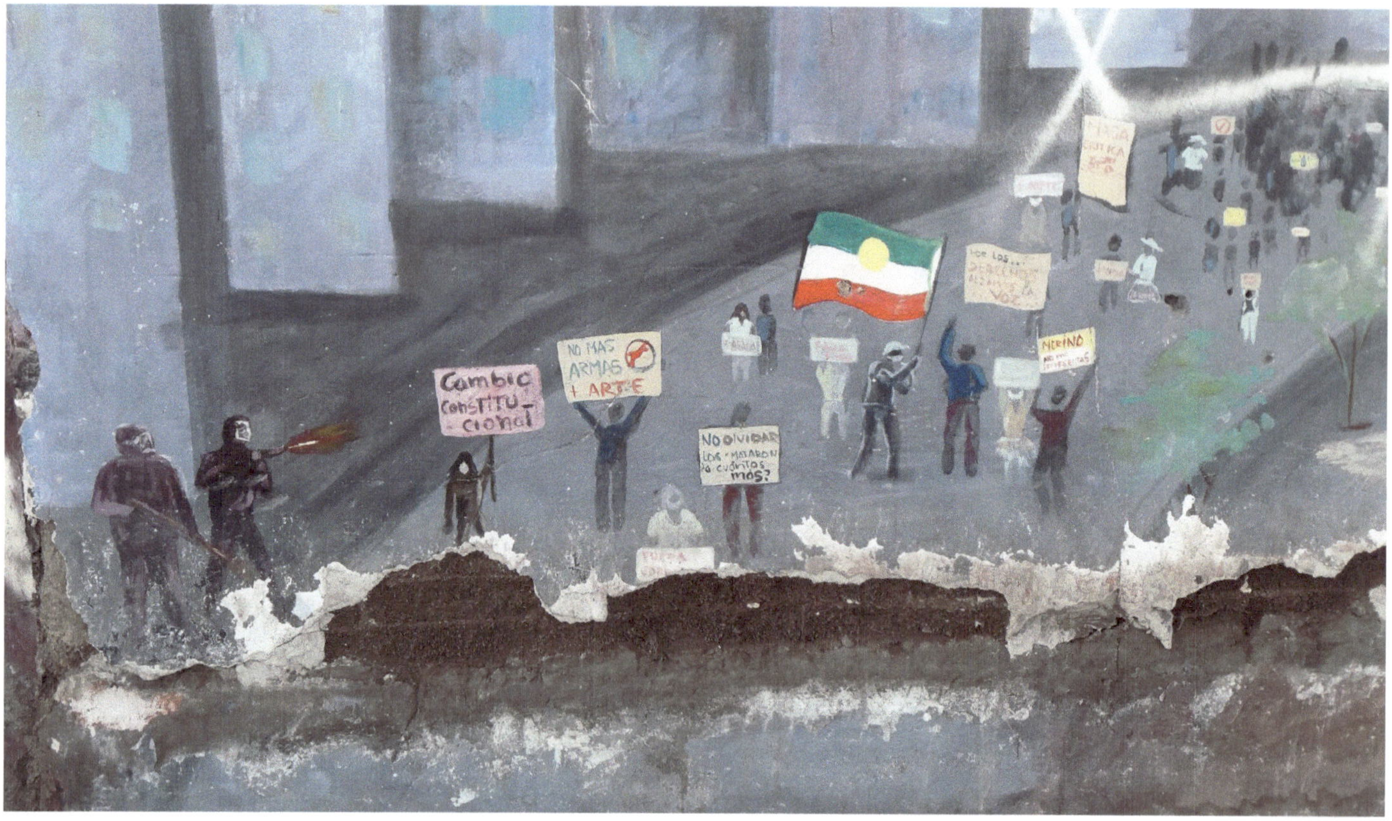
Cambio constitu-cional
NO MAS ARMAS + ARTE
NO OLVIDAR
LOS MATARON
¿a cuántos más?
MERINO

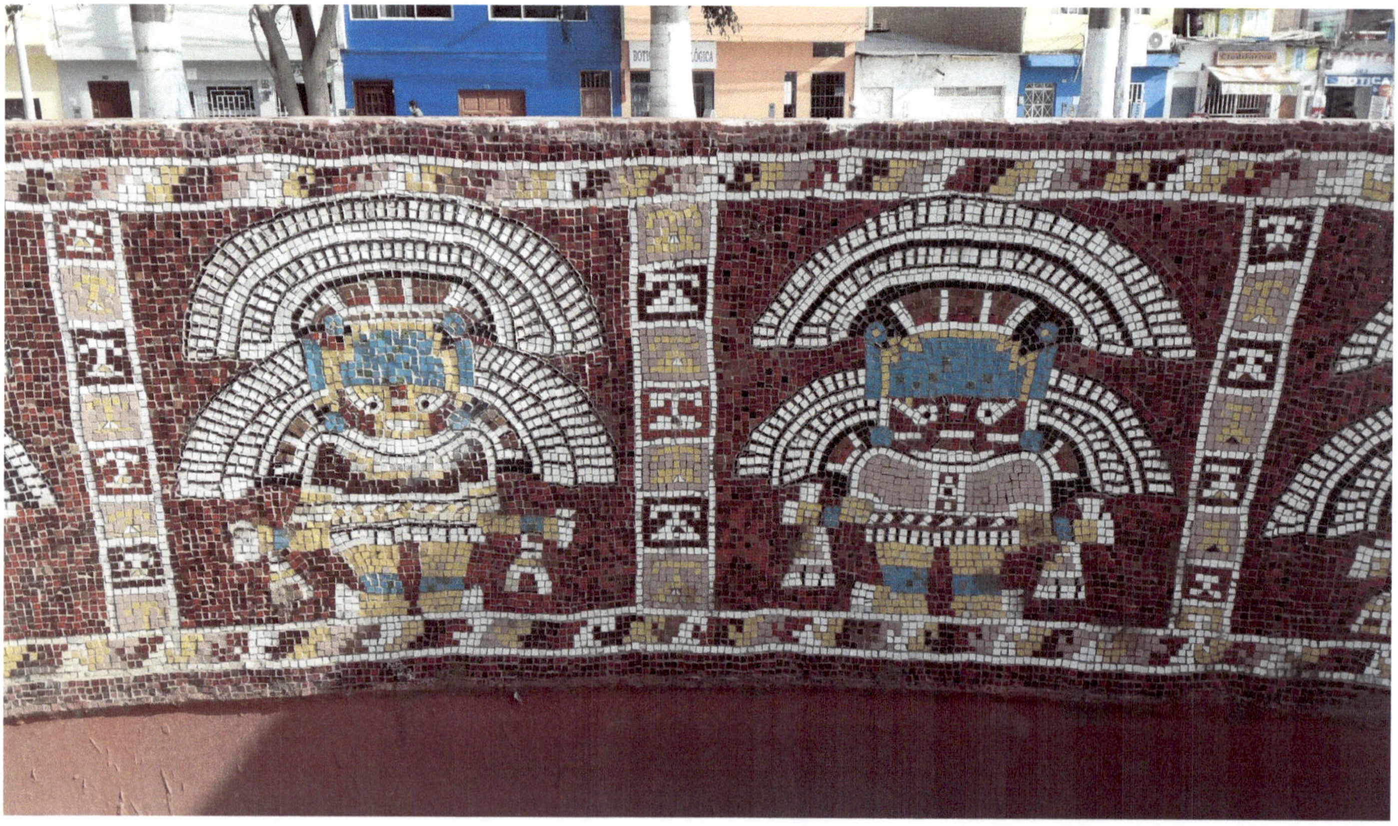

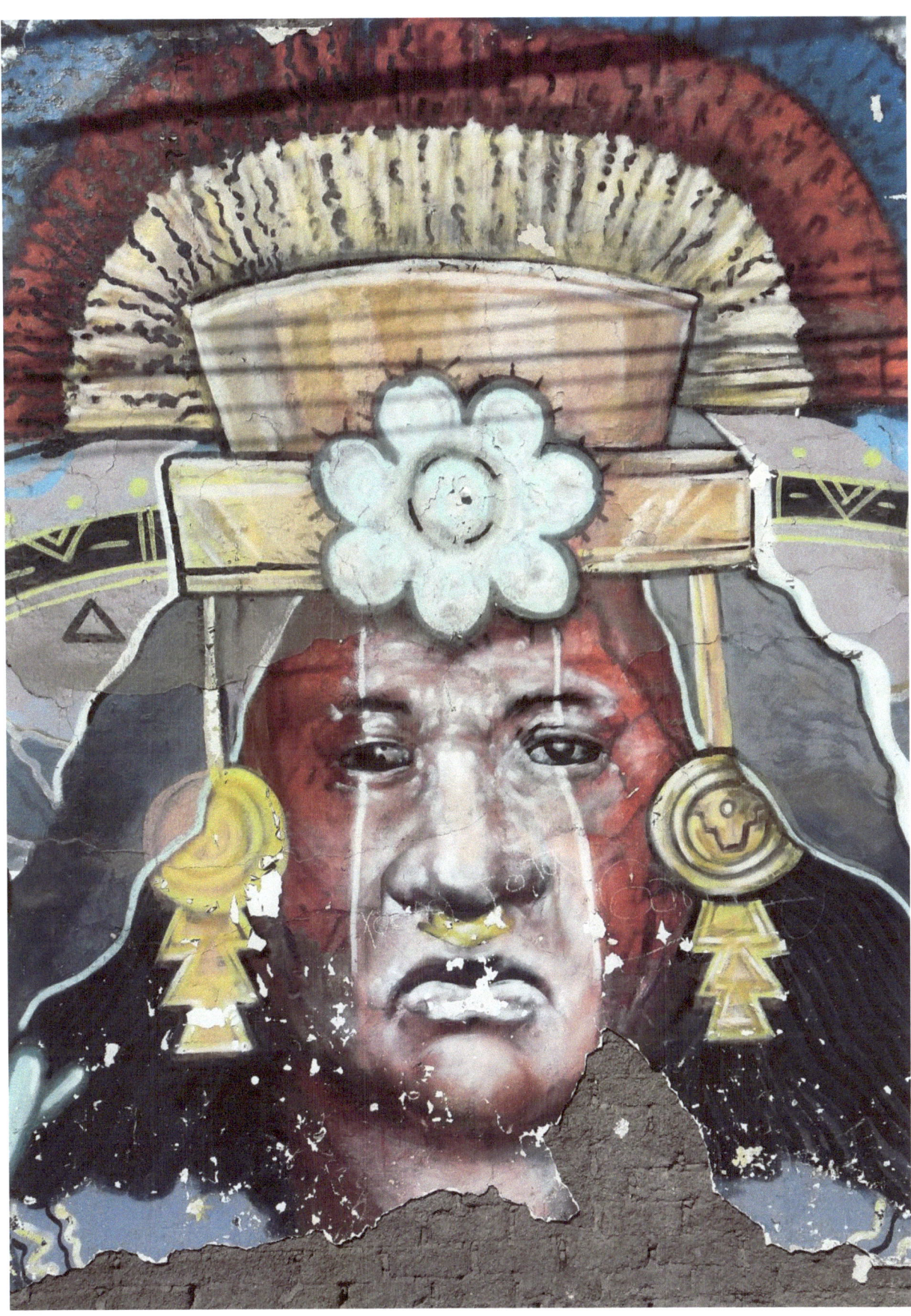

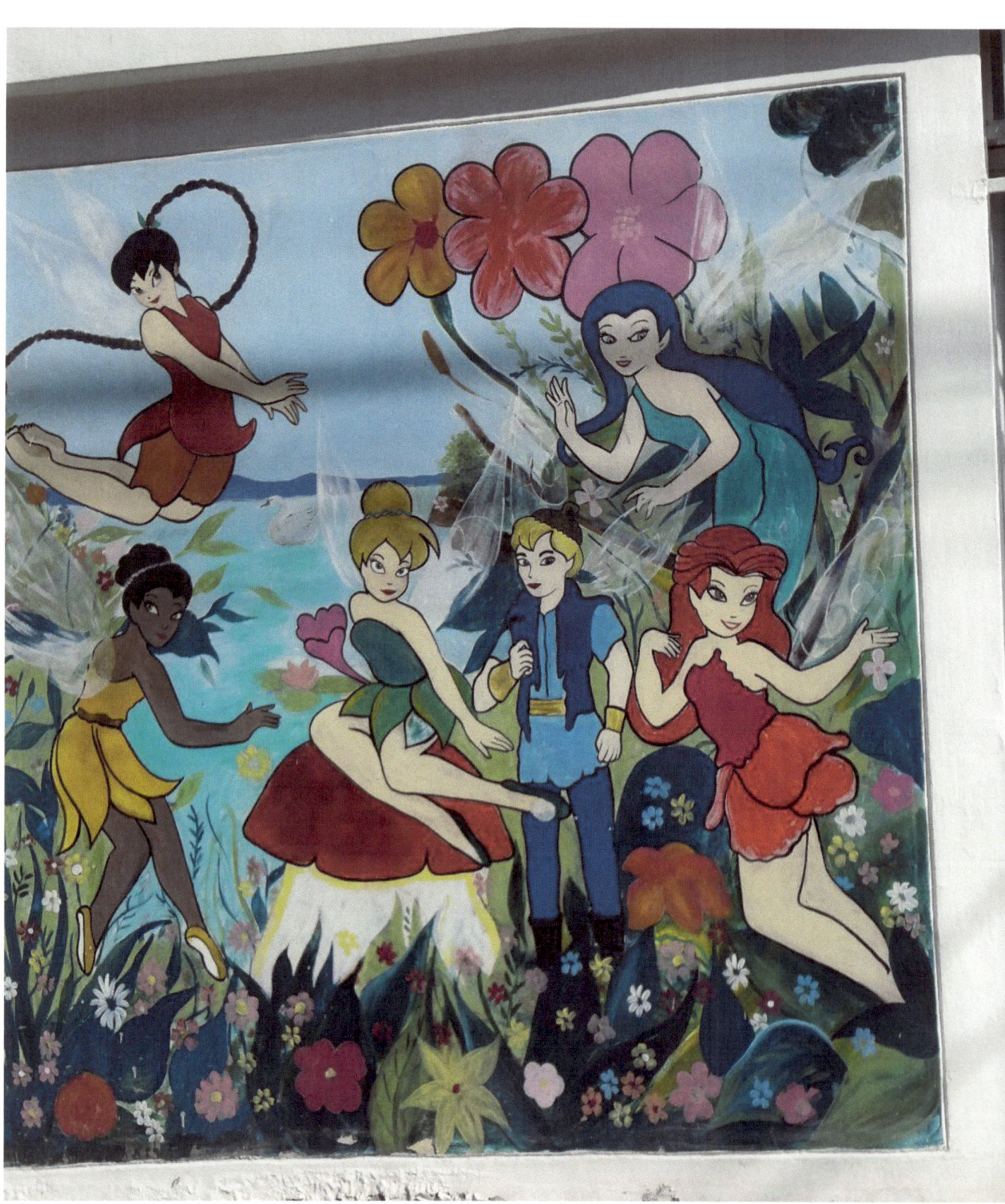

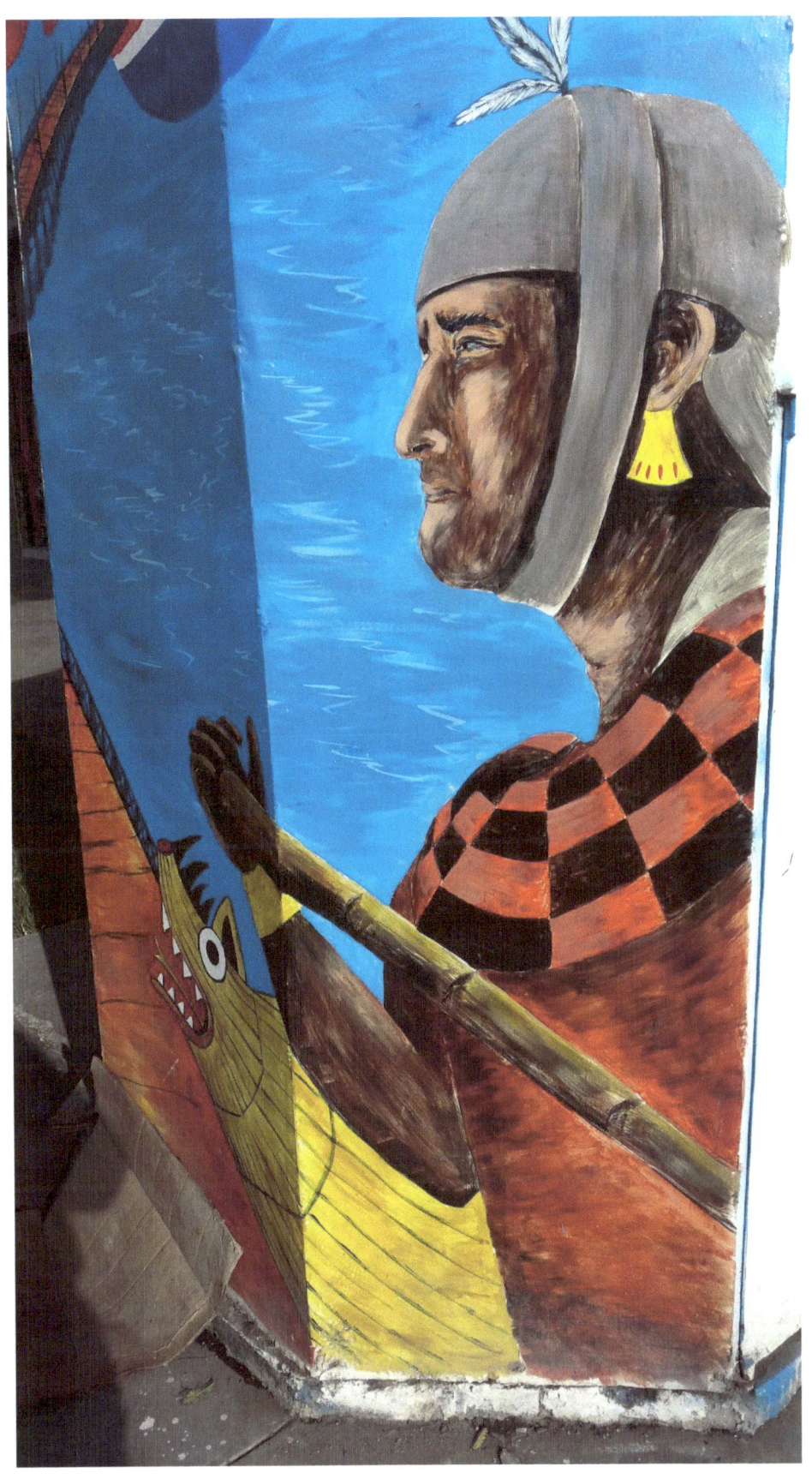

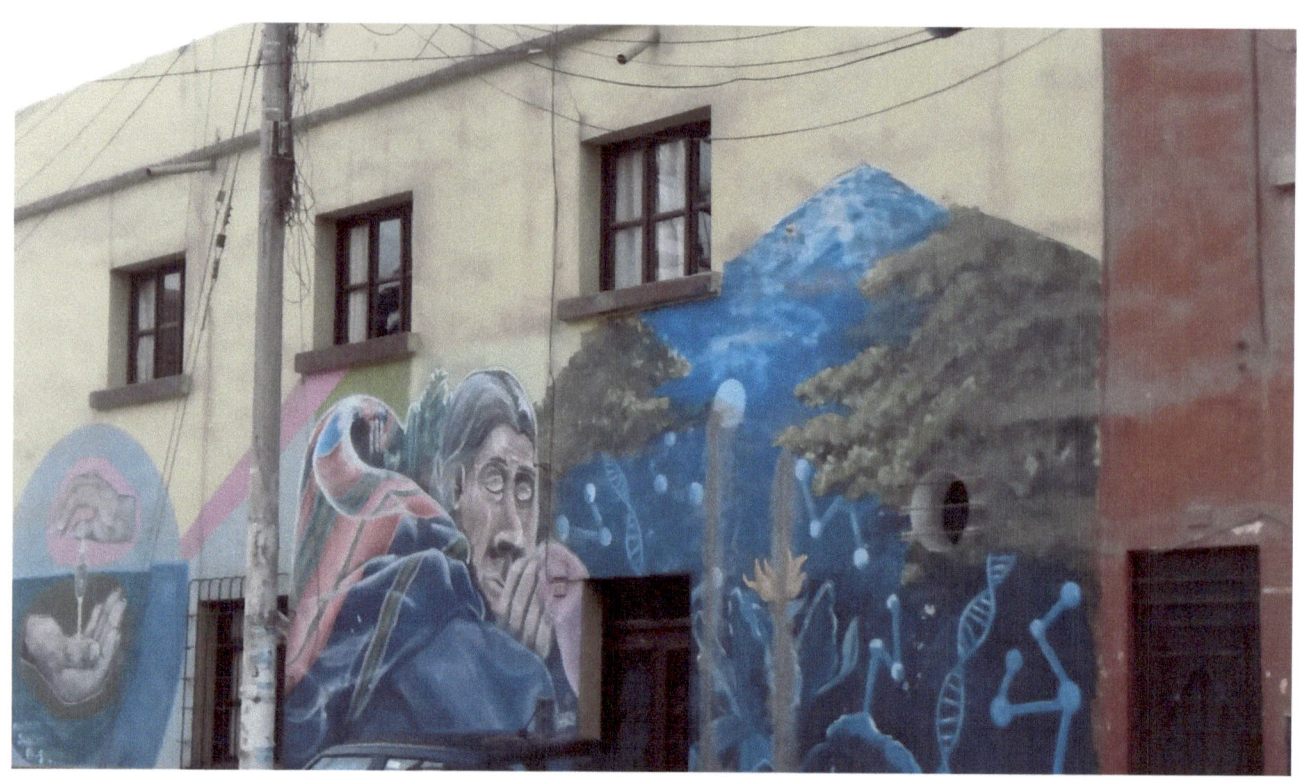

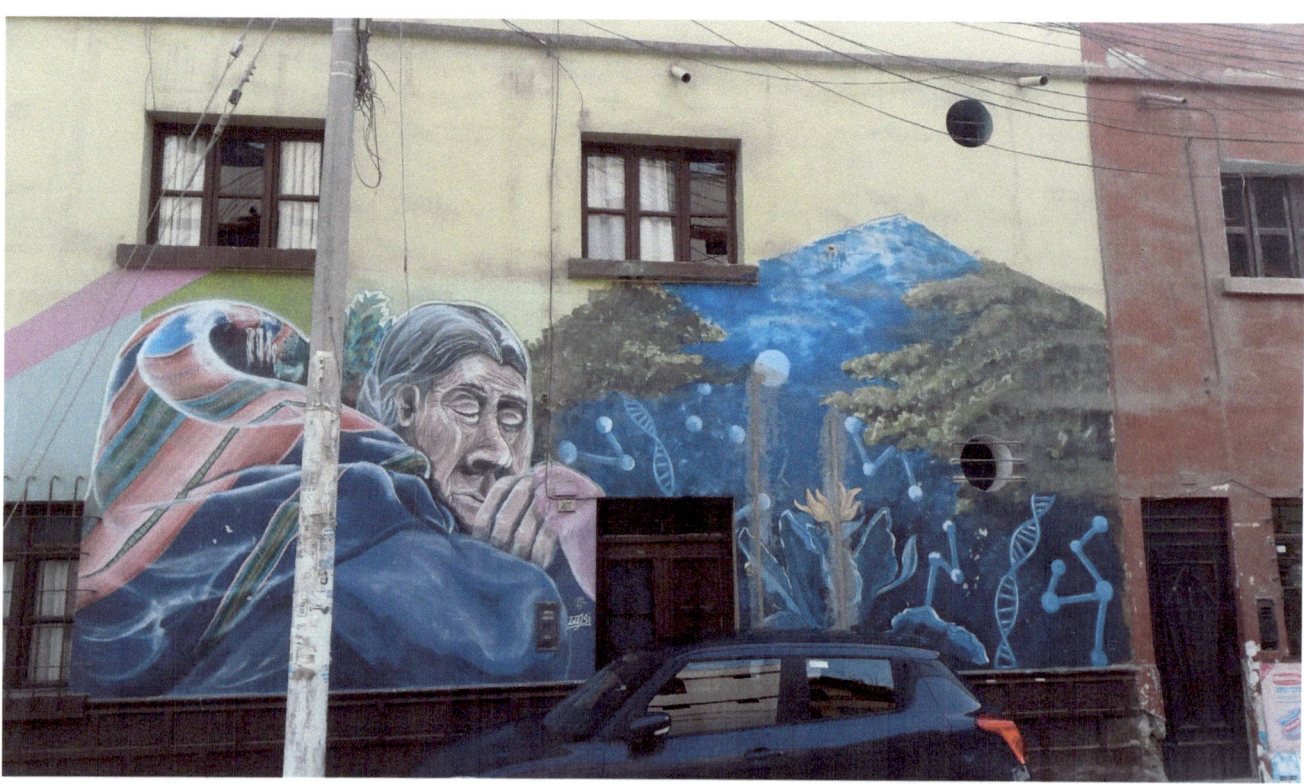

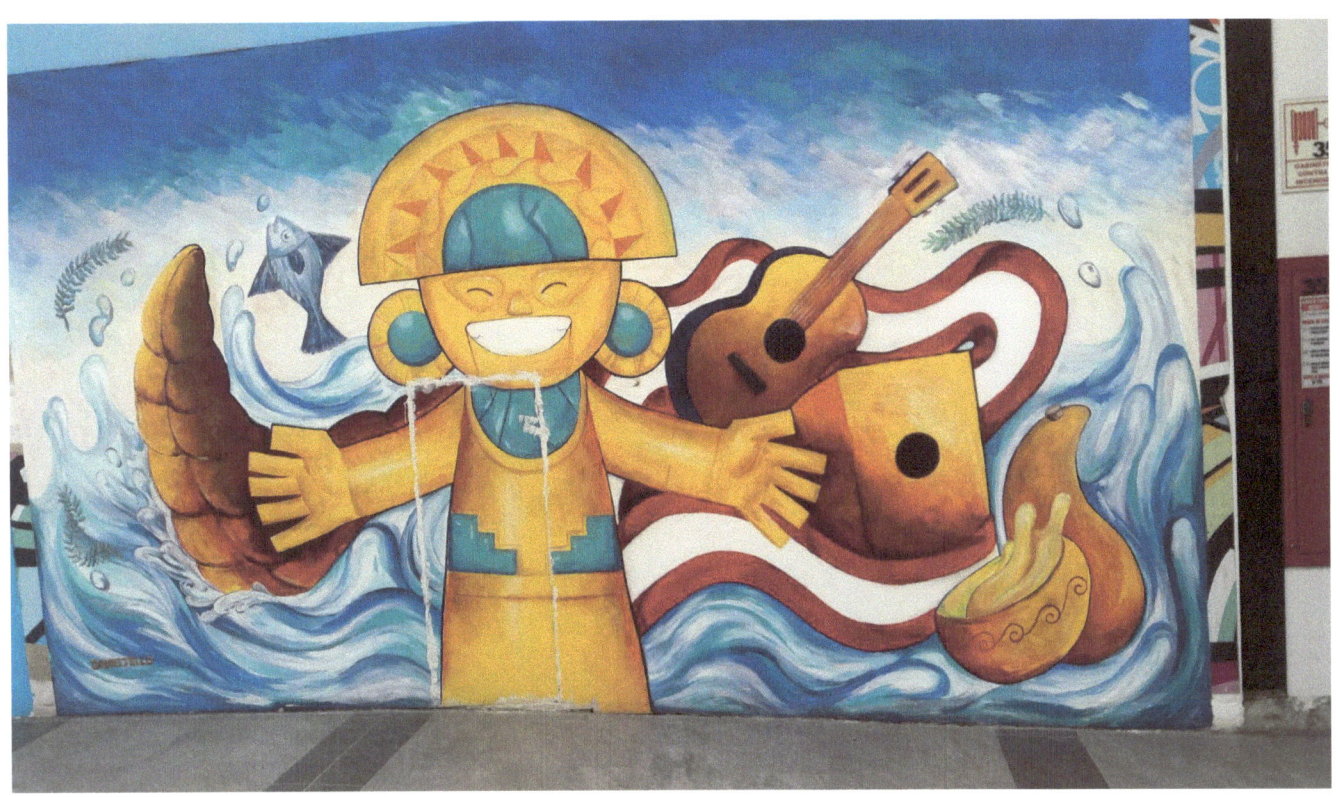

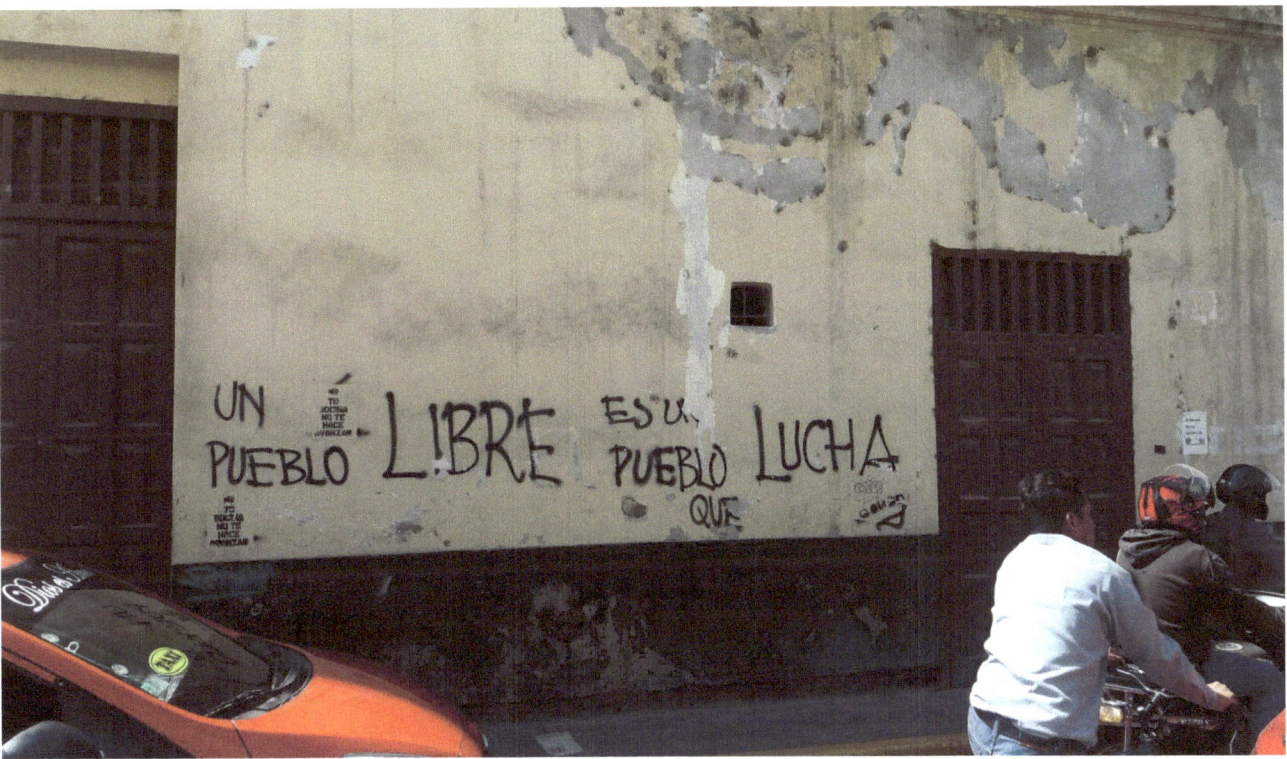

A free Pueblo is a Pueblo that fights for it

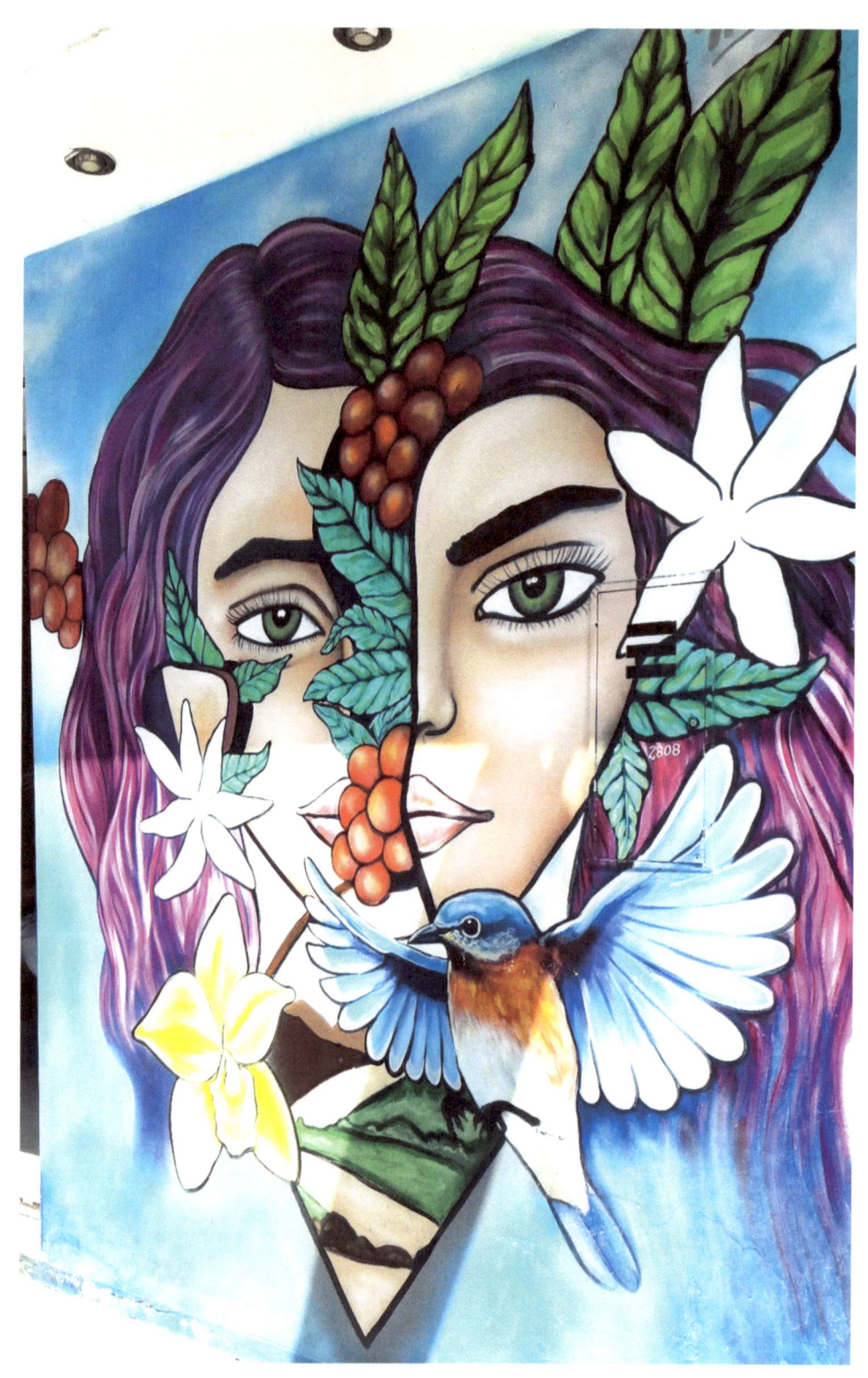

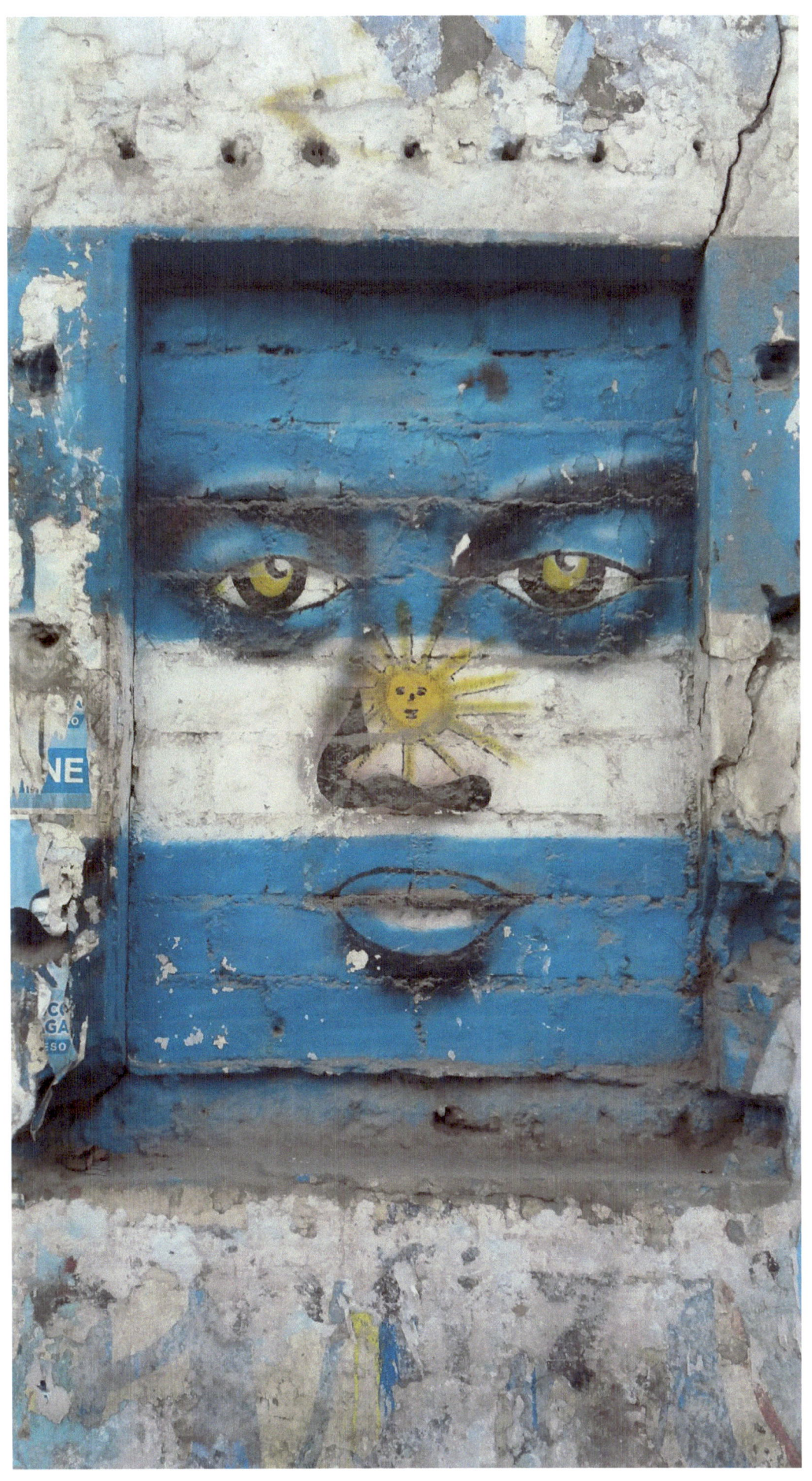

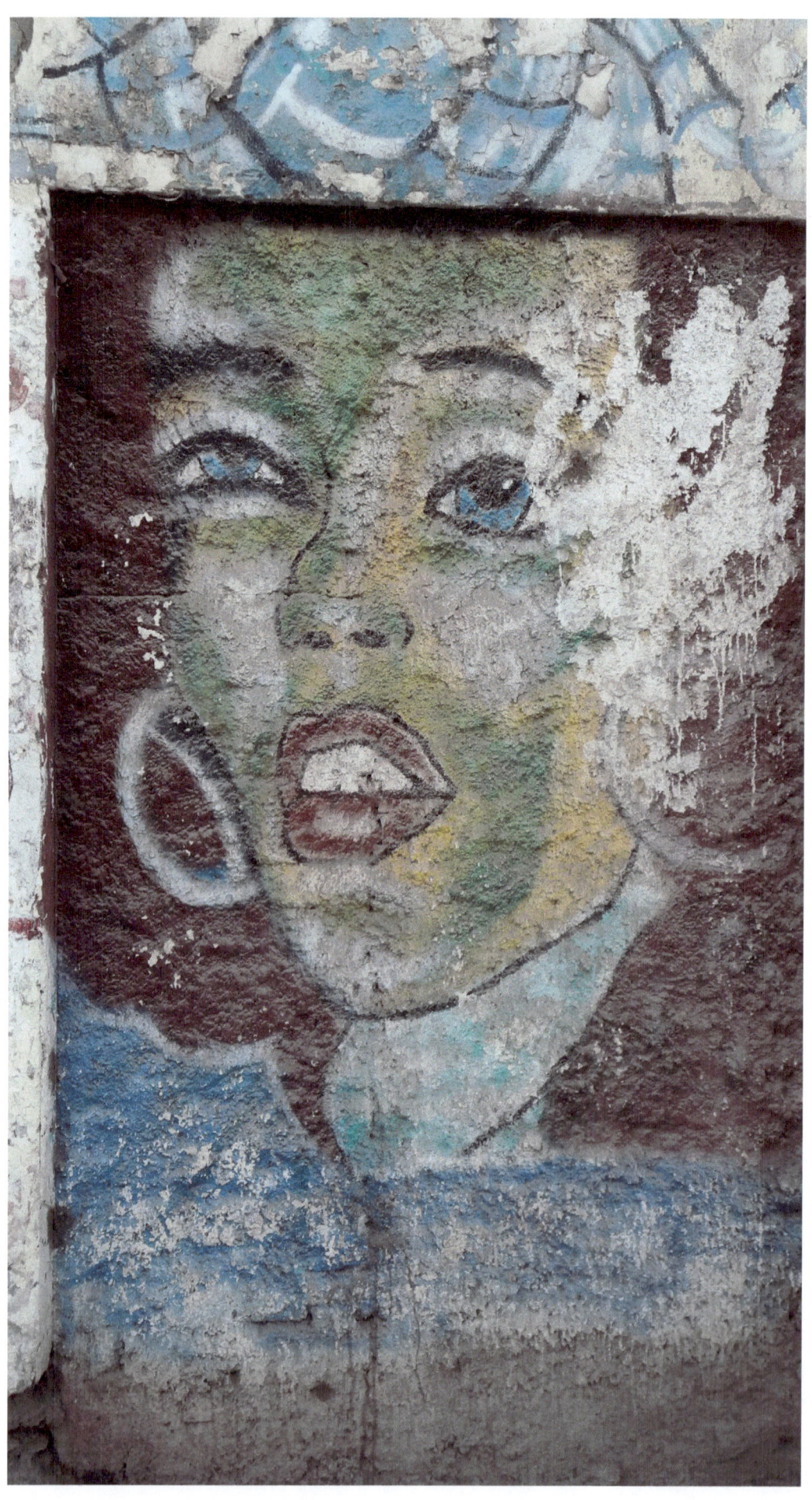

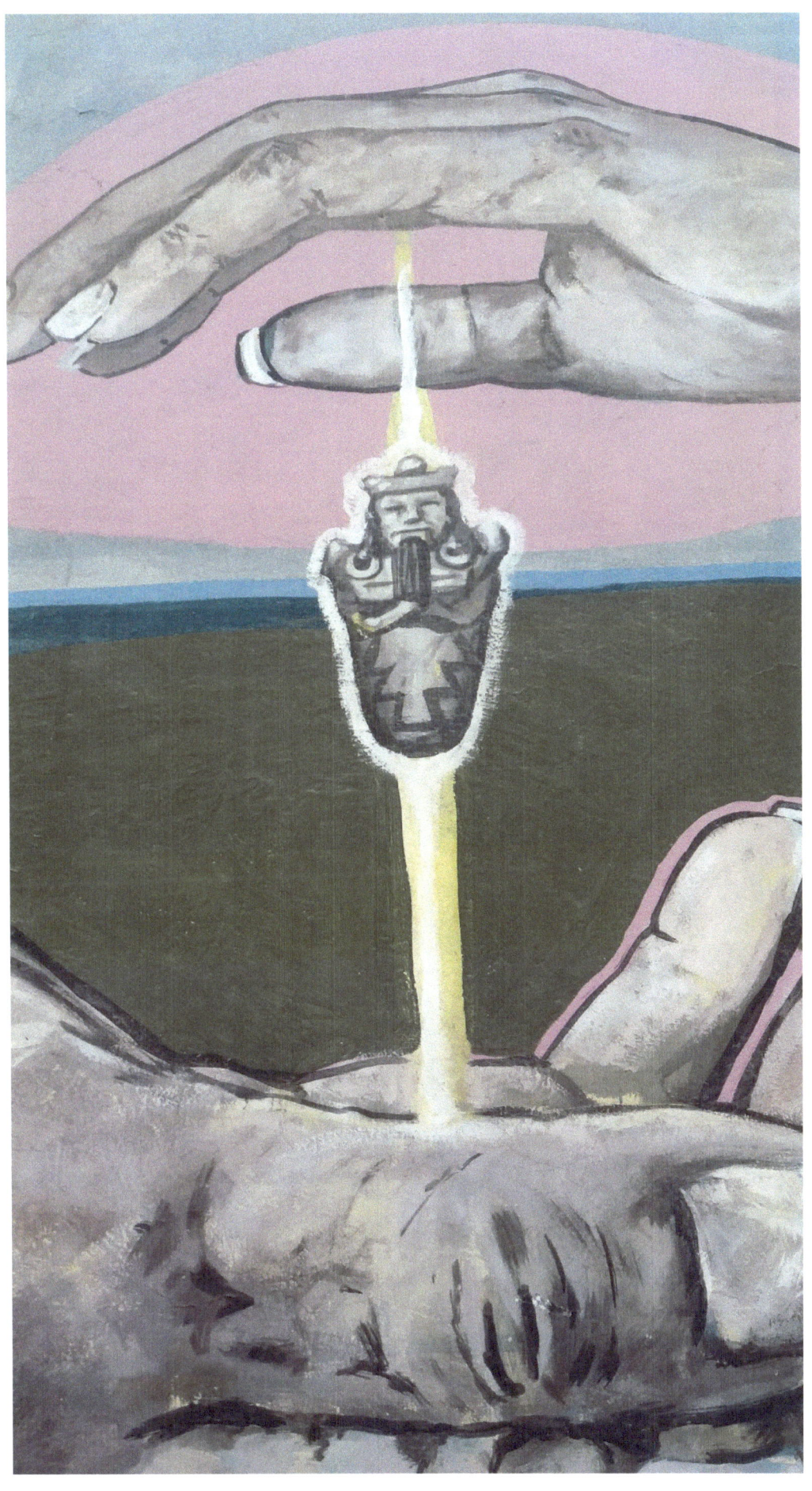

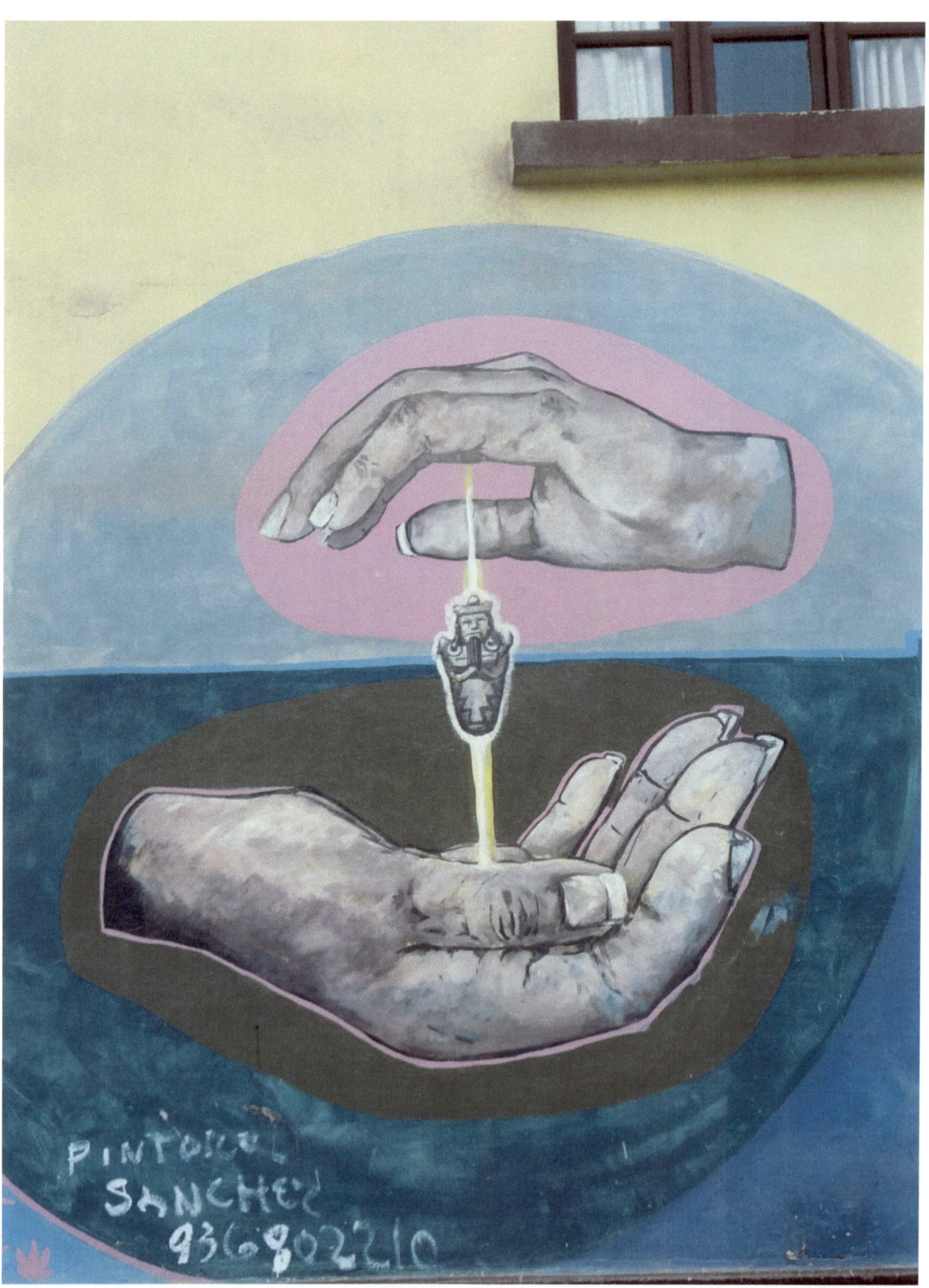

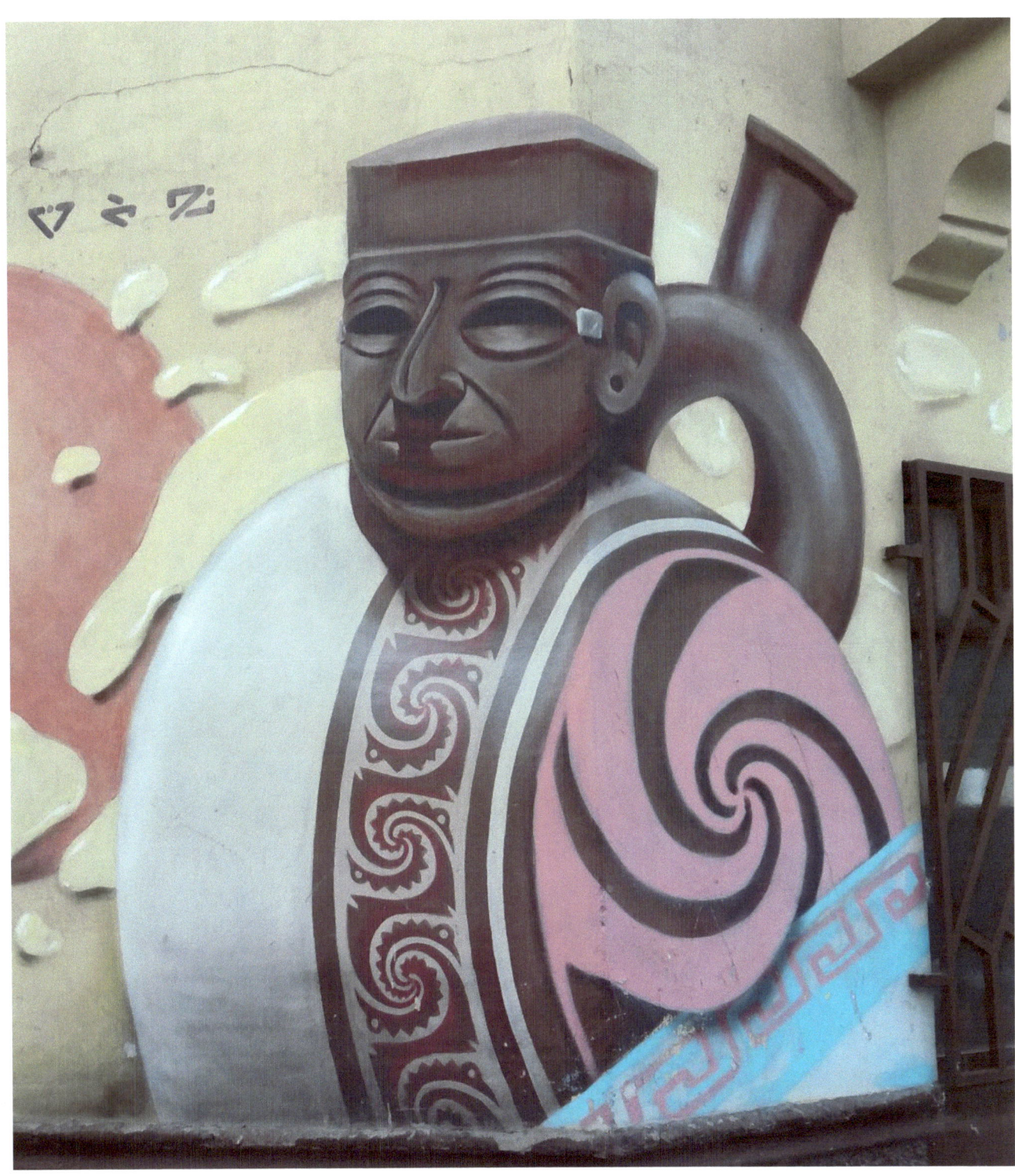

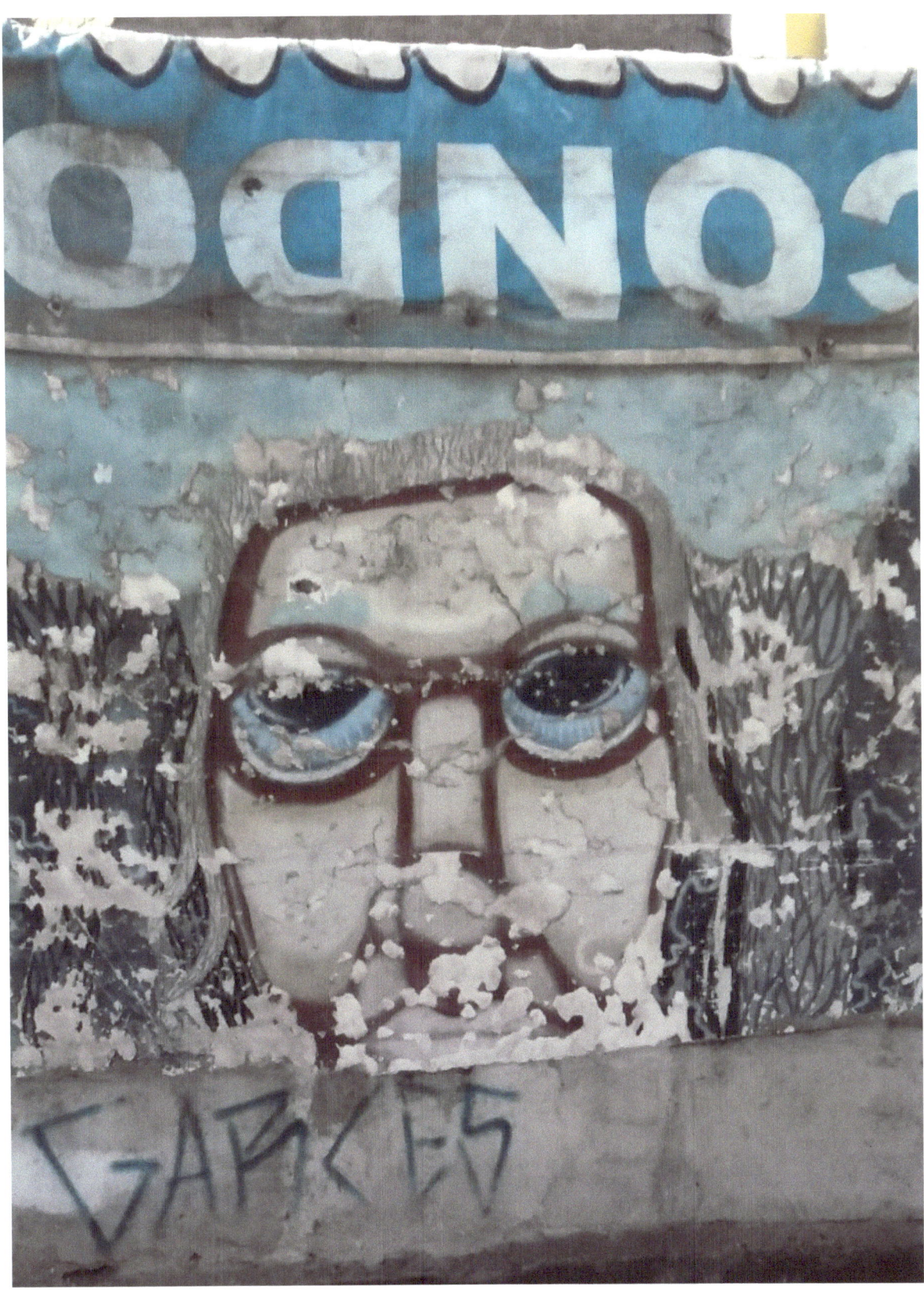

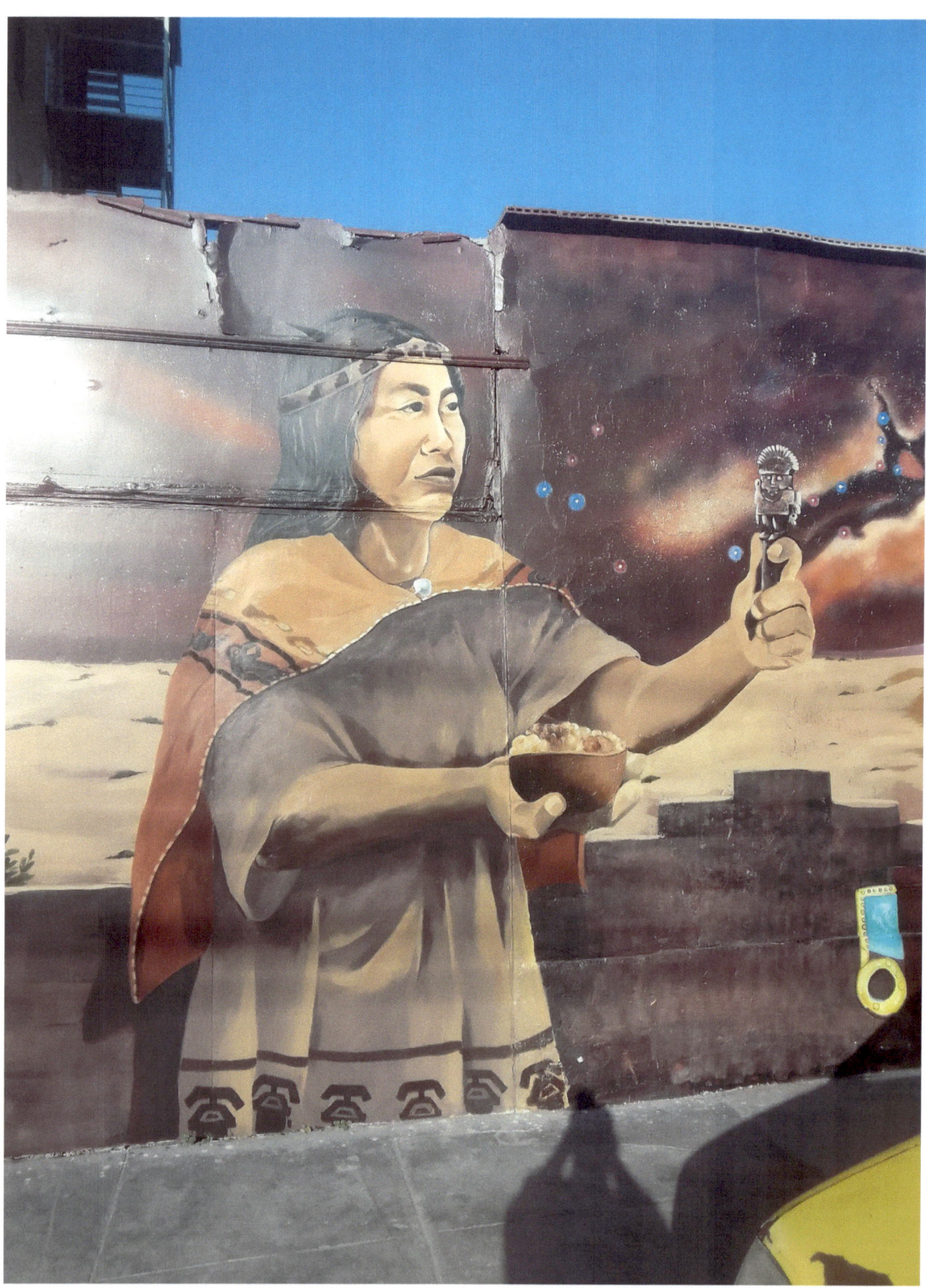

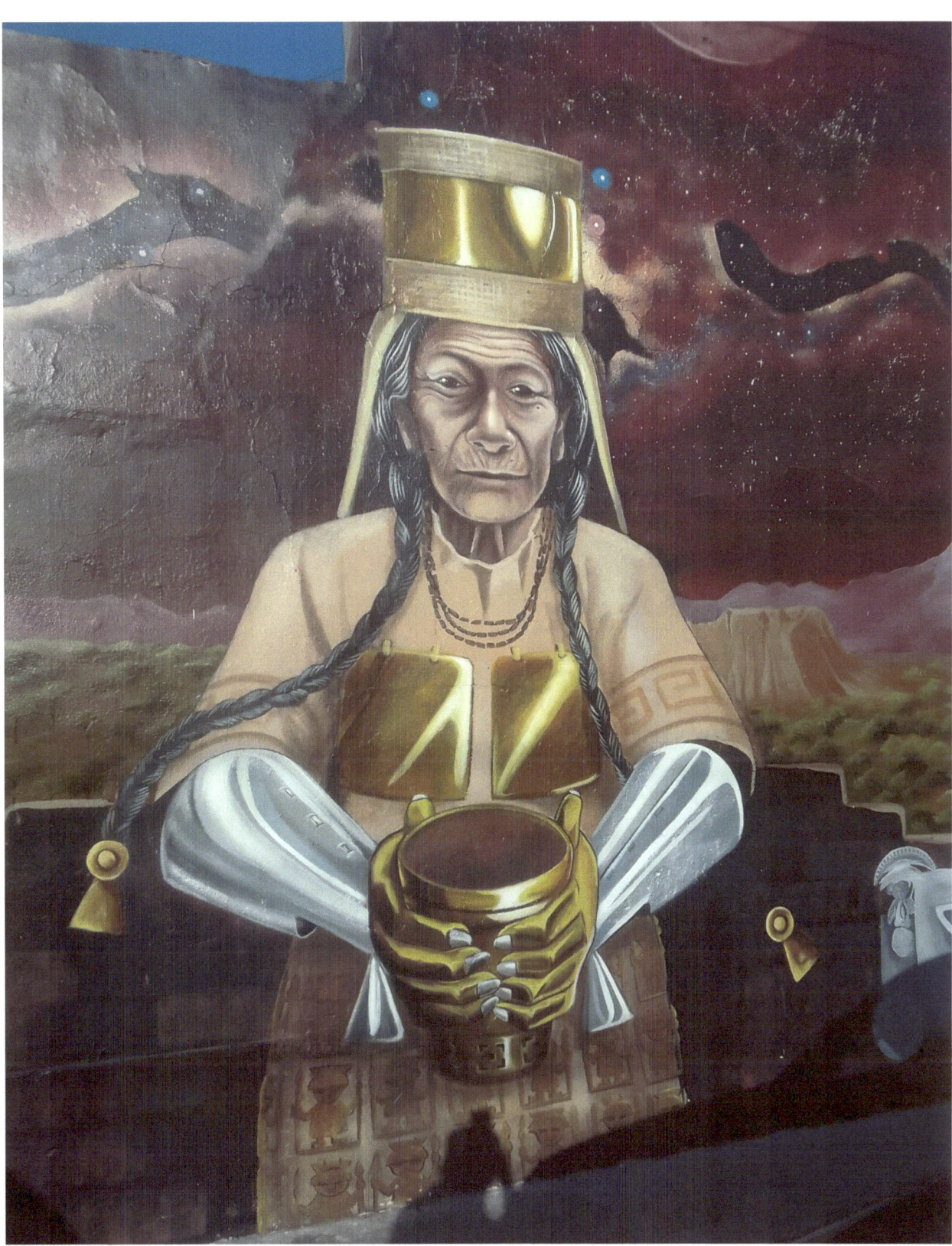

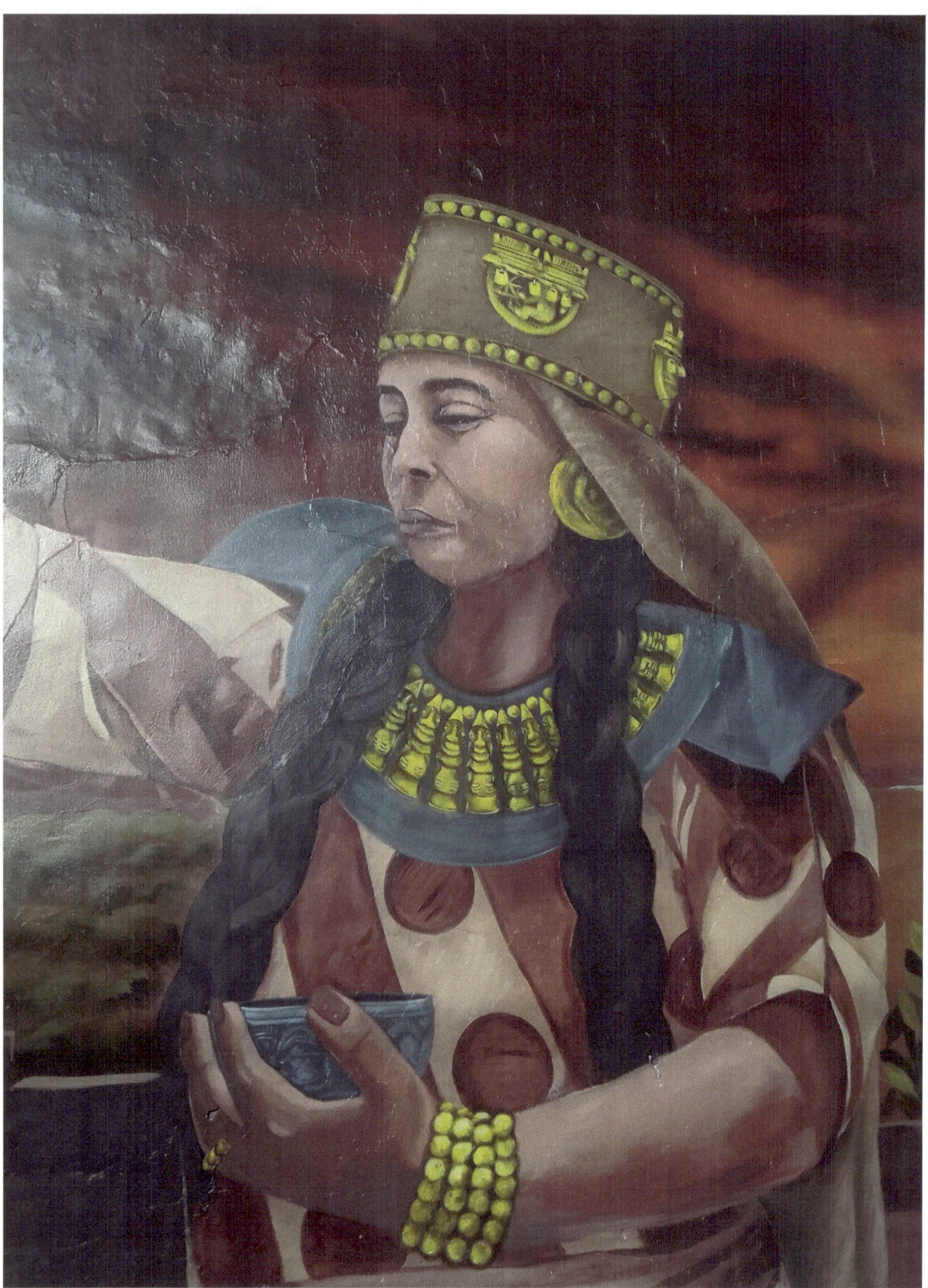

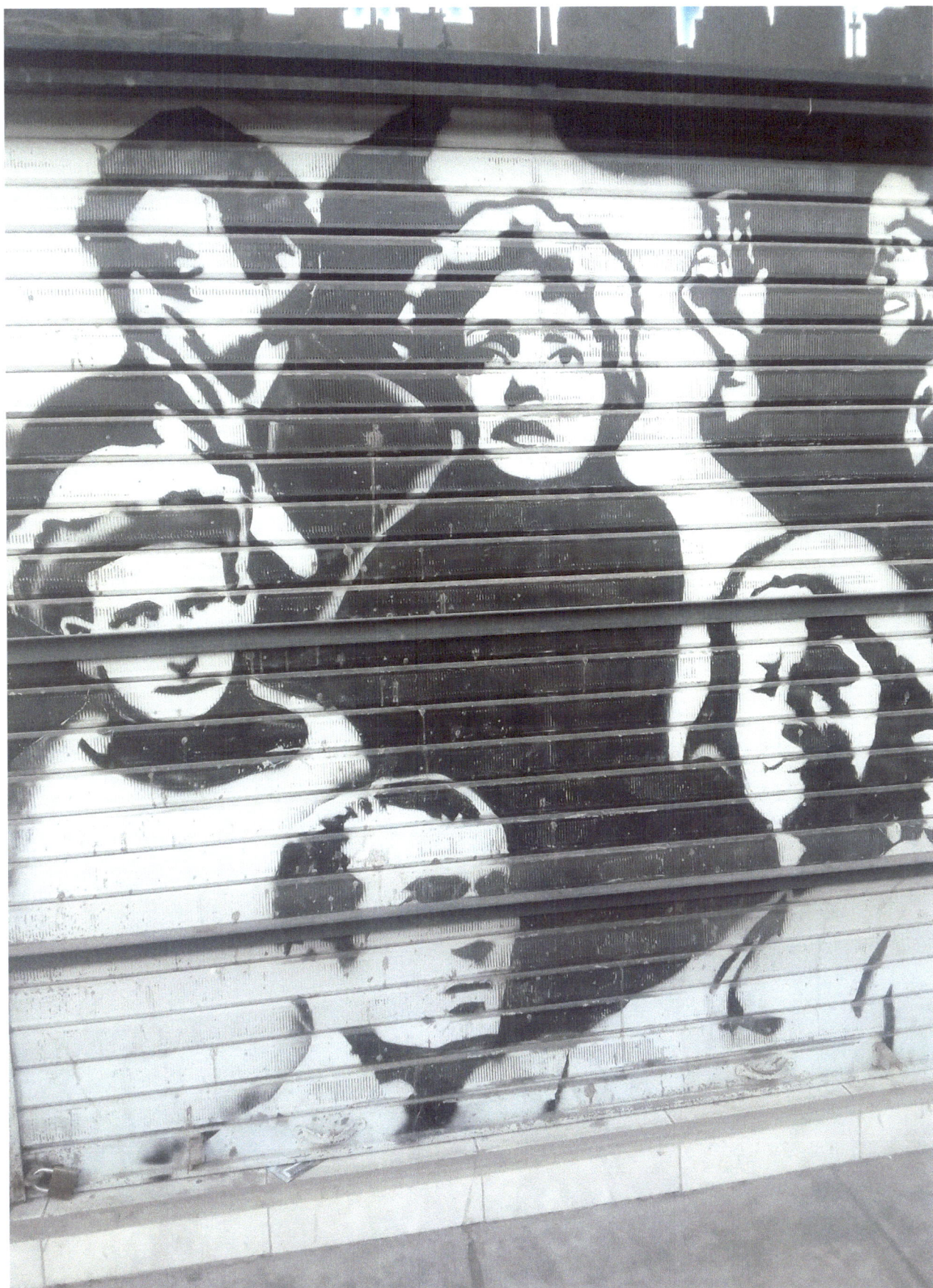

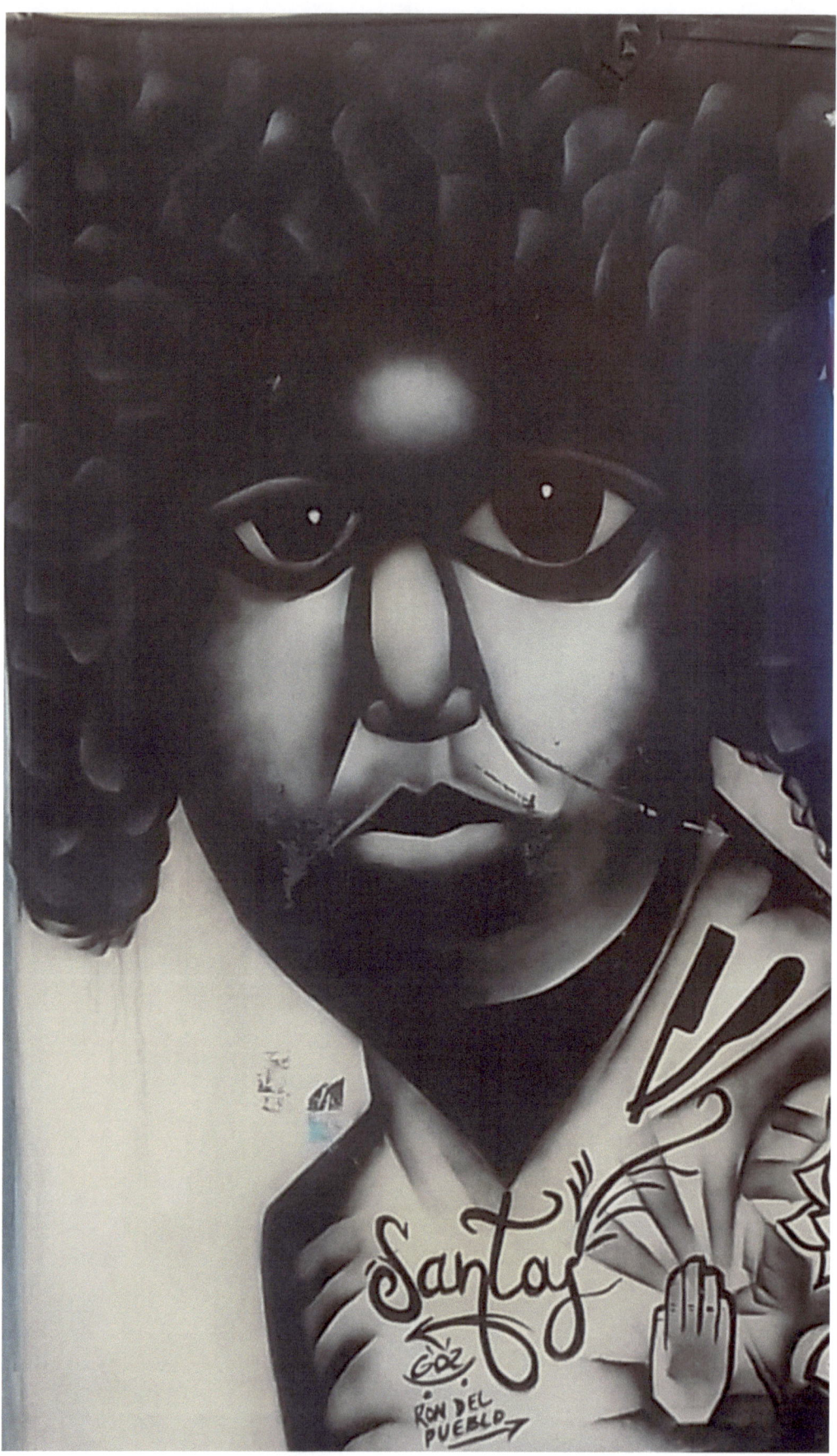

Thank you for looking at our book

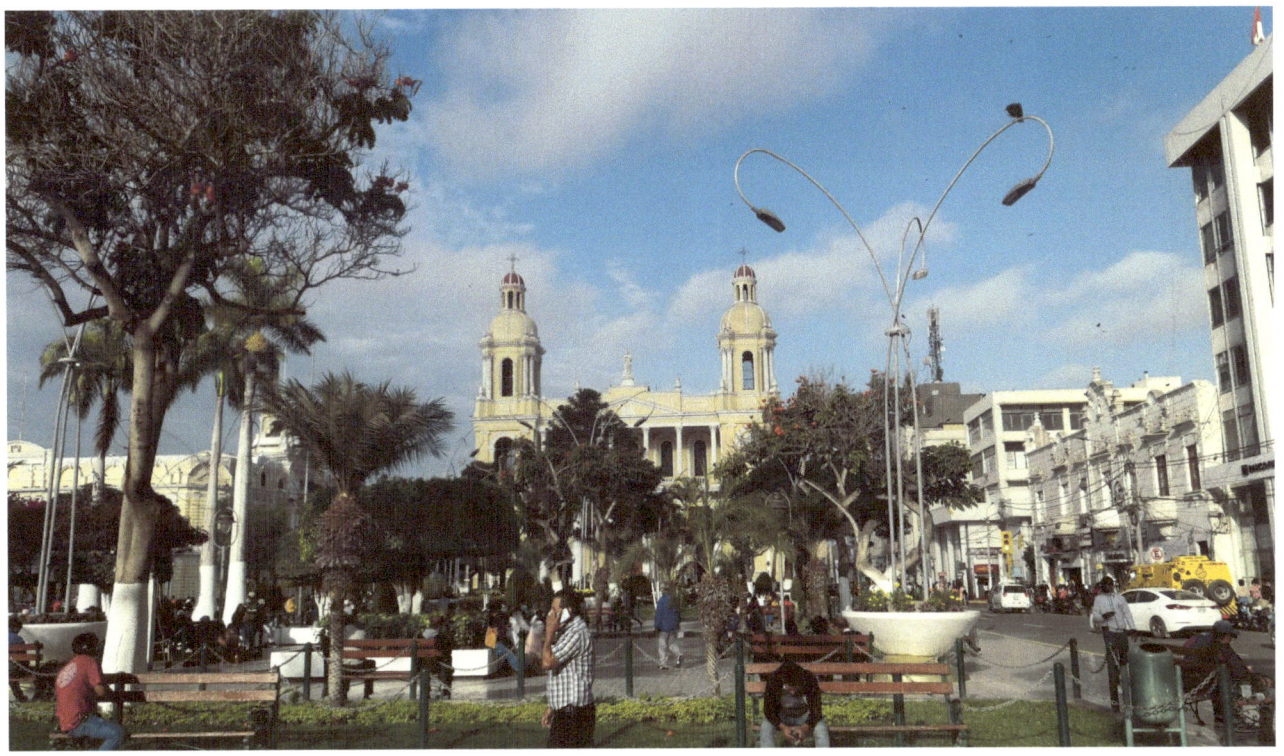

Chiclayo Street Art

Photos from Chiclayo, Peru

By Wesley Gibbs

Questions, Comments, Corrections, Advice,

Please contact Walking The Ceiling Publishing at

BogotaBook@gmail.com